Moving into the Superintendency

Other Titles of Interest by Rowman & Littlefield Education

Stepping into Administration: How to Succeed in Making the Move
by Thomas A. Kersten

Success in the Superintendency: Tips and Advice
by Kay T. Worner

School District Master Planning: A Practical Guide to Demographics and Facilities Planning
by Kelley D. Carey

The Future of School Board Governance: Relevancy and Revelation
by Thomas L. Alsbury

Financial Accounting for School Administrators: Tools for School
Third Edition
by Ronald E. Everett, Donald R. Johnson, and Bernard W. Madden

Moving into the Superintendency

How to Succeed in Making the Transition

Thomas A. Kersten

Published in partnership with the American Association of School Administrators

ROWMAN & LITTLEFIELD EDUCATION
A division of
ROWMAN & LITTLEFIELD PUBLISHERS, INC.
Lanham • New York • Toronto • Plymouth, UK

Published in partnership with the American Association of School Administrators

Published by Rowman & Littlefield Education
A division of Rowman & Littlefield Publishers, Inc.
A wholly owned subsidiary of The Rowman & Littlefield Publishing Group, Inc.
4501 Forbes Boulevard, Suite 200, Lanham, Maryland 20706
www.rowman.com

10 Thornbury Road, Plymouth PL6 7PP, United Kingdom

British Library Cataloguing in Publication Information Available

Library of Congress Cataloging-in-Publication Data

Kersten, Thomas A.
Moving into the superintendency : how to succeed in making the transition / Thomas A. Kersten.
p. cm.
Summary: "Moving into the Superintendency: How to Succeed in Making the Transition provides novice superintendents with the knowledge and skills needed to succeed in their new roles. Thomas Kersten, a highly experienced school administrator with eleven years of superintendent experience, shares the most practical and useful strategies that will help new superintendents optimize their early successes" --Provided by publisher.
ISBN 978-1-61048-436-7 (pbk.) -- ISBN 978-1-61048-437-4 (electronic)
1. School superintendents--United States. 2. School management and organization--United States. 3. School management and organization--Vocational guidance--United States. 4. Educational leadership--United States. I. Title.
LB2831.72.K47 2012
371.2'011--dc23
2012011129

Printed in the United States of America

Contents

Foreword

Within the first sixty days of becoming a superintendent, I faced four career-shaping challenges. How I responded to each would mold my superintendency, establish my relationship with my new board of education, define my relationship with the teaching staff and the union, and test my resiliency. What resources were at my command? Who could I turn to for advice and assistance? Was I prepared for these challenges or not?

Twenty-four hours into my superintendency, my predecessor informed me that a district employee faced an FBI criminal investigation. Because of the immediacy of the news, it was my responsibility to inform the board and to lead the district's response to the situation. Before I was able to unpack my books and organize my desk, my leadership was tested.

My second major challenge was to immerse myself into highly complex and contentious negotiations with our teachers' union. One year before I became superintendent, the district experienced its first strike, resulting from the district's increasingly bleak financial picture and the teachers' desire to stand their ground. This conflict was made even more unpredictable due to the volatile personality of a most unique board member. As superintendent, I served on the board's negotiating team. Yet, in the context of these intricate and prolonged negotiations, I met and began to form a crucial professional and personal relationship with the union president.

A third task, prosaic by most accounts and unrelated to my educational mission, was to supervise the completion of a water drainage project on our athletic fields. This project deeply frustrated the board and presented its own pitfalls and personalities.

Finally, as this first summer unwound, one of our teachers was involved in a near-fatal car accident. She required a medical leave and a replacement teacher for her classroom. As the new school year hastened in our small school district, I knew that responding well to her, properly handling the mechanics of the leave request, and filling this crucial vacancy were crucial to the smooth start of the school year.

So, what resources were at my command? To whom could I turn? Was I prepared? In retrospect, I wish that, prior to embarking in my new position, I had had the sound counsel and advice found in Tom Kersten's book, *Moving into the Superintendency*. Some who attempt to write such books are ego-driven braggarts. Others come off as too cute or overly simplify the complex. On the other hand Kersten is the "real deal," merging sound, down-to-earth suggestions and current research. As a successful principal, assistant superintendent, and superintendent in highly demanding districts, Kersten honed his craft. While succeeding as an administrator, Kersten pursued educational writing. In retirement Kersten became a professor of educational administration with a passion for improving the practice of administration through sound research and excellent teaching.

In Kersten's *Moving into the Superintendency*, I could have found clear advice to face my challenging first sixty days. In chapter 6, "Establishing Relationships Within the School District," Kersten would have counseled me to pay attention to establishing relationships with all staff in the district. When faced with complex dilemmas, Kersten would have encouraged me to realize my limits and seek the advice of those with greater expertise than me in their respective fields. His perspectives on school board relationships, chapter 5, and on working smarter, chapter 11, and on "Getting Off to a Successful Start," chapter 3, would have simplified my learning curve, reassured me when I was on the correct path, and reoriented me when I strayed into a dead-end canyon. With guidance found in his book, I could have reduced the amount of "trial and error" learning that I (and most new superintendents) experienced.

Easy to read and replete with real-life examples, this book has much practical wisdom without being formulistic. To use a sports analogy, unlike those golf devices that "guarantee" a lower score, Kersten's suggestions point to a better "golf swing" with the full knowledge that transitioning well into the superintendency is like lowering one's golf score in that it takes intelligence, planning, effort, measured strides, and nimble footwork. As in golf, where every lie is different and every shot unique, the transition into a new superintendency has its individual contours, challenges, and trials. Kersten's steady advice is a resource worth acquiring.

Nelson Armour, EdD
Retired superintendent;
Adjunct professor, Roosevelt and Loyola Universities

Preface

Making the Decision to Seek the Superintendency

From the time I was appointed to my first administrative position as an assistant middle school principal in my twenties, I began thinking about the superintendency. What triggered my thoughts was my superintendent. From the onset, he was someone I admired. He was well respected and presented himself as a self-confident, in-charge leader. He seemed to have a dream position.

Yet, as I gained more administrative experience through principalships in different school districts, my initial interest began to waver. For the first time, I saw some of the realities of district leadership. I watched as my superintendents became the targets of staff, parent, and school board criticism. I observed various community factions make personal attacks on them during public meetings. In fact, on those occasions during which I was invited to closed sessions of the board, I observed how some board members would challenge the superintendent and attempt to micromanage the district. As is often the case, I soon discovered that things tend to look much better as an outside observer.

During one of my principalships, I remember having a conversation with our assistant superintendent about his personal ambitions. He was a highly competent, well-respected people person who I assumed would soon move up the administrative ladder to the superintendency. When I asked him if he was considering becoming a superintendent, he looked at me and said, to my surprise, that he was not willing to take the job security risk. He went on to describe the complexity of the position and how our current superintendent, who I saw as a master politician, even struggled at times. Slowly, I watched as my administrative ambitions began to shift from the superintendency. Soon thereafter, when asked if I wanted to become a superintendent, I started telling people that I was not sure.

Before long, I decided that the assistant superintendency was for me. As a central office administrator, I was fortunate to work with a strong, confident superintendent who had previously retired after a long career as a superintendent in another state. As his assistant, I had the opportunity to observe him closely. To some degree, he made the position appear less daunting. However, I still watched as he wrestled with frequent challenges from both inside and outside the organization. Although I became more confident in my abilities, I was still not sure whether the superintendency was for me.

My perspective began to change three years into my assistantship when our superintendent announced his retirement effective the following year. Suddenly, I found myself in the position of deciding if I would be a candidate. Of course, he strongly encouraged me while faculty members and staff lobbied me to apply. What ultimately forced my decision was the thought that I might have to work for someone with whom I would not be comfortable. I had watched similar scenarios play out in neighboring school districts, sometimes with undesirable results.

After an extensive search process, I was appointed the superintendent. That was when reality hit. After all the former superintendent's retirement activities concluded, I found myself on my own. I knew that there was no turning back. Within three weeks, I experienced my first solo school board meeting. As colleagues related later, I came across as nervous and somewhat unsure. Fortunately, I worked with solid administrators and reasonable school board members who were not too judgmental.

To my surprise, over the next couple of years I learned that the superintendency was actually much more manageable than I had previously thought. I soon discovered that, even though I had increased responsibilities, I also had more authority and greater freedom to structure my day. In retrospect, many of my early career fears were proven unwarranted.

Over those first years, I worked hard to succeed, often relying primarily on intuition and judgment rather than actual knowledge. I also was fortunate to have been hired into a district with a long history of administrative stability, which allowed me the luxury to learn on the job.

Yet, what I also realized later in my career was that I could have been much less of a trial and error decision-maker if only I had more knowledge about transitioning into the superintendency. With better preparation, I could have substantially shortened my learning curve and avoided some pitfalls, which I unintentionally created for myself. If I had known more about how to navigate that first crucial year, I could have stepped more smoothly into the superintendency.

This book, *Moving into the Superintendency: How to Succeed in Making the Transition*, is a practical guide for aspiring and practicing superintendents who want to increase the likelihood of having a successful, long-term career. It is based on my many years of superintendent experience, as well as interviews with numerous superintendents from urban, suburban, and rural school districts.

Acknowledgments

To write a book, an author must depend heavily on the assistance and guidance of many others. I am truly indebted to several individuals who helped me move this book from a series of initial ideas to press. Each willingly gave of their personal time and professional expertise. Just as important, they encouraged me through their personal support without which this book may never have been published.

Above all, I want to thank my wonderful, talented wife Beth who served as a source of ideas, a peer reviewer, and an editor for the three books I have published to date. As a highly experienced and successful central office school administrator, her insights and critiques have been invaluable to me. Even though she is extremely busy, she is always there when I need her.

During the past few years, in particular, I have come to rely on my good friend and fellow superintendent, Nelson Armour, for his guidance. As a former principal and later superintendent colleague, I have always respected Nelson's knowledge, judgment, and advice. In addition, I have valued his willingness to peer review my writing and provide me with needed reality checks. His forthright evaluations and his additional ideas helped enrich this book.

Finally, I want to thank four additional friends/professional colleagues. I especially want to recognize my friend Lee Snyder who volunteered to edit the manuscript. Lee, who actually works in the world of finance, has a special expertise in editing. His technical support was invaluable in enhancing this book's readability. Finally, three superintendents or former superintendents, Frances McTague, Don White, and Joe Pacha, served as peer reviewers. I want to express my gratitude to them for all their help.

ONE

Assessing Your Fit for the Superintendency

As a school administrator, one of the most important personal and professional decisions you will ever make is whether to move up the administrative ladder. For some individuals, this means the principalship. Others are motivated to seek central office positions, while a select group aspires to the superintendency. No matter what your career choice, each position has its own unique challenges and subsequent rewards. Each requires specific skills, some of which are more critical at one administrative level than another.

A key to succeeding as an administrator is assessing your match for a particular position so you do not find yourself in a position for which you are not a good fit. It is important to remember that, just because someone was successful as a principal or central office administrator, this does not necessarily translate into success as a superintendent. Do not be afraid to rely on your intuition. If a superintendency does not feel right, as hard as it might be, you should walk away from it.

UNIQUENESS OF THE SUPERINTENDENCY

In some ways the superintendency is different from other administrative positions. It requires certain talents and skills that may not be as crucial to success as a principal or even another central office position. As a consequence, those aspiring to become superintendents should consider the following differences between the superintendency and other administrative positions, some of which may be more of a matter of degree. By realistically weighing your personal talents, skills, and aspirations against the unique features of the superintendent's role, you can begin to assess whether the superintendency is the best fit for you.

Superintendents Must Be Comfortable with Ambiguity

Because superintendents deal regularly with what Sigford (2005) calls dilemmas, that is, situations without simple solutions, they must accept that ambiguity is a common element of district leadership. Although all administrators face dilemmas, those at the district level are often more broad based and publicly visible.

Superintendents who were former principals tend to be especially adept at solving school-based problems. As principals, they learned how to manage student discipline issues, stay on top of day-to-day management problems, and negotiate the politics of teacher class schedules. However, now as superintendents, they find themselves frequently facing much more complex challenges often devoid of the simple or quick-fix solutions characteristic of school-level leadership.

Consider, for a moment, these typical superintendent dilemmas.

- Student enrollments are increasing rapidly but only in one area of the school district, which also happens to be in the lowest socioeconomic section. Parents and teachers at this school are raising concerns about fairness, equity, and overcrowding. However, other district parents, including some school board members from the "wealthier" side of town, are content. They do not face overcrowding and see no advantage for their children should a boundary change occur. Rather, they prefer that the school board take whatever actions necessary at the overcrowded school as long they have has no impact on them. If it does, look out!
- Student test scores continue to remain flat even though the school district has invested heavily in support programs, professional development, and outside services. Nothing tried to date has improved student performance. School board and community members are beginning to question the effectiveness of the district's leadership. Public questions are surfacing about the superintendent's ability to lead school improvements efforts.
- The school district's budget deficit is growing quickly. The state is not fully funding public education due to the sluggish economy. Expenditures are projected to continue to outpace revenues even though the district has made substantial expenditure reductions in recent years. Soon the district will be faced with extremely difficult program and staff reductions unless there is an infusion of new revenues. Unfortunately, the mood of the community is clearly "no new taxes."

These are the types of dilemmas that fall squarely on the shoulders of superintendents who are expected to solve the apparently unsolvable. What is interesting is that successful superintendents look at these ambiguous dilemmas as challenges rather than roadblocks. They are not afraid to confront such issues head-on, even if they know there is some chance that they might not survive the process. As a potential superintendent, you have to ask yourself if you can accept the uncertainties that are inevitable in district leadership and remain motivated to lead problem-solving efforts.

Superintendents Are Expected to Lead Their Districts in Times of Crises

Any superintendent knows that it is impossible to predict and plan for every crisis. On the calmest of days in the least controversial school district, anything can happen. Someone can phone in a bomb threat on a windy, twenty-below-zero-degree day, a student could brandish a weapon during class, or the local police could appear at one of your school offices to arrest a teacher for unlawful sexual conduct.

Superintendents must be prepared to respond quickly, calmly, and rationally. They have to have the knowledge and skills to make the right decisions, sometimes with little or no notice. As a new superintendent, you must learn to expect the unexpected and be comfortable taking charge of such situations.

Do not be afraid to lead. You will make mistakes but also learn from them. Those who are reticent, afraid to make the wrong call, or overly dependent on others to make crisis decisions for them may exacerbate rather than manage such complex problems. When you assume the superintendency, you should recognize that you must always be willing to assert yourself in any crisis situation.

Superintendents Live in a Highly Political Environment

Superintendents must be adept political leaders. They are expected to be congenial to everyone from the taxpayer watchdogs to disgruntled parents to demanding union representatives. When confronted with unwarranted criticism, angry public challenges, and backdoor comments, they must present themselves as calm, friendly, concerned leaders. When everyone else is "losing their cool," they have to be the calmest person in the room.

Mishandling any issue may have a much more detrimental effect on the superintendent's career than at a lower administrative level. As a consequence, when considering the superintendency, you have to assess your political savvy. The best way to do so is to reflect on how you have responded to such difficulties up to this point in your career.

Ask yourself questions such as:

- When you were a building administrator, how did you handle aggressive students and parents?
- When disgruntled parents challenged some decision you made, did you become angry?
- Did you usually find ways to diffuse potential political controversies so they remained at the building level?
- Have you been able to develop the personal political skills necessary to negotiate challenging situations?

All administrators deal with politics. The difference is that political issues at the superintendent's level tend to be much more visible and often impact the broader school community.

Superintendents Need to Be Decisive Decision-Makers

Have you ever worked for an indecisive leader? Although some employees may at times grumble about administrators who are overly direct, the reality is that most want a single individual "in charge." This does not mean an authoritarian dictator, but rather someone who is a strong and yet collaborative leader.

School districts that lack decisive leadership at the superintendent level can quickly lose their focus and direction. When there is a leadership void, it is quickly filled by others. Superintendents who are indecisive create voids that may be filled by school board members, other administrators, and/or teacher union representatives. Often these individuals or groups have self-serving agendas and may even compete against each other to assert their positions.

In a very short period of time, a school district's entire culture can change from one of certainty to uncertainty. If you have ever worked in a school district where a strong, well-respected superintendent retired and was replaced by one who was not, you saw firsthand the effect of indecisive leadership.

Most often this form of leadership will result in school board micromanagement. Before long, board meetings lose focus. Meetings extend to midnight or later. Audience participation is permitted to increase, sometimes even during the board's discussion of business items. Board member participation shifts from a consensus to competitive focus.

Although this can occur even under the leadership of an effective superintendent, it is exacerbated in a leadership void. As you consider the superintendency, you want to assess your comfort level with decisive decision-making. Unlike elementary principals, who may succeed even if they are less direct, superintendents are held to a different standard. Their "bosses" are elected officials, not school employees, and are more likely to make demands and assert themselves into any number of district activities.

Superintendents Must Have Especially Thick Skin

All school administrators must come to grips with the fact that they cannot please everyone. They must have "thick skins" to recognize that conflict and criticism are inherent in school leadership (Kersten 2010). What distinguishes the superintendency from other administrative positions, though, is the level of community visibility.

Building-level administrators regularly experience criticism. However, most public comments are confined primarily to the school or individual school community. At times, they may filter up to the district office, but normally not much beyond.

As a superintendent, you must be prepared to face internal as well as external criticism, some of which may become personal. Since many superintendents live within the school district boundaries, their children attend district schools. As such, when superintendents are criticized, their families often feel the effects. Polka and Litchka (2008) in their book *The Dark Side of Educational Leadership: Superintendents and the Professional Victim Syndrome* provide vivid examples of the challenges and criticisms superintendents must endure.

Today with instant media access and constant person-to-person communication, superintendents are often subject to regular public scrutiny. Any comments they make may be posted on YouTube or text messaged throughout the community almost instantly.

Superintendents who have "thick skins" are less likely to overreact to professional and personal criticism. They recognize the importance of thinking before speaking or acting. Because they know that public criticism is unavoidable, they learn to disassociate themselves from it on a personal level and recognize it as job embedded. As you consider your fit for the superintendency, you need to assess your tolerance for criticism. You must be able to distance yourself from the effects of criticism that is inherent in school district leadership.

Superintendents Must Accept That They Are Not Always the Ultimate Decision-Makers

Although superintendents must be decisive, they must also accept the reality that they are not always the ultimate decision-makers. They function as the chief operating officers of public entities. Superintendents know that some decisions are made exclusively by the school board. As a result, they may offer advice and counsel to the ultimate decision-makers, school board members.

Periodically, superintendents find themselves having to publicly support decisions with which they may personally disagree. Have you ever been employed in a school district where the board of education made decisions such as those below?

Scenario 1: A group of high school seniors decides to organize a "senior ditch day" two weeks before graduation. In recent weeks, the principal made several public announcements warning that anyone who participated in such an activity would be suspended from school and commencement. Undeterred, two dozen students disobey the order. True to his word, the principal enforces the consequences. However, the school board president's child and several friends are part of the group.

Soon after the suspension decision, the school board president calls for a full board discussion of the consequences. After a brief debate, the school board overrules the suspensions as too harsh and reinstates the students. The superintendent is placed in the position of justifying the change to the principal, staff, and parents.

Scenario 2: The school district is facing personnel and program cutbacks due to growing financial concerns. In such situations, the superintendent generally takes a leadership role in educational program recommendations. Under the direction of the superintendent, the administration leads a process to gather expenditure reduction suggestions from a large segment of the school community. Most of those who choose to participate are the most active parents and teachers. Each tends to focus on their personal interests. Members of the school board are clearly aligned with the active parent group.

As informal superintendent/school board member communication unfolds, it is apparent that programs that benefit the "haves" are considered untouchable. In the end, the board decides to maintain all sports, instrumental music, and gifted programs. Those for lower ability students and less visible clubs and activities are dramatically reduced.

In addition, a boundary change, which is in the best interests of district students, is rejected. Even though the superintendent lobbied board members for the change, pressure from politically connected parents stalls the effort.

In the end, the superintendent is left to explain these decisions to the school community. Any comments construed as unaligned with the board could put the superintendent's job security on the line.

Before accepting a superintendency, you need to consider that you could easily find yourself faced with similar dilemmas. Remember that, although you are hired by a particular school board, its makeup can change quickly. When board members leave, you must be prepared to adjust to the changed board or be prepared to consider a new position.

Superintendents Are Expected to Deal with Public Officials and Politicians

For most administrators, their contact with public officials and politicians is usually associated with children or school-related activities. Similar to any other parents, these community leaders have children in local schools. In addition, they interact with school-level administrators around school activities, award programs, and community service activities.

Although superintendents, too, have parent-related contact with community leaders, they more often interact with them around political or other less popular issues. Superintendents often find themselves negotiating intergovernmental agreements on such topics as facility usage or tax increment financing districts. Superintendents quickly learn that dealing with public officials is different from school employees. Many have boards of their own. Others compete with them for scarce tax dollars. At times, superintendents must be prepared for the inevitable "political ego."

As you weigh your fit for the superintendency, consider whether you are the type of person who relishes this role. Can you see yourself fitting into a community-based political structure? Are you willing to spend evenings and weekends meeting with governmental representatives, often arguing a point for which others have little sympathy? Do you have the political savvy to work with individuals with strong egos without responding competitively?

The Superintendent Has No District Peers

One of the adjustments new principals must make is to the loss of the peer networking they enjoyed as teachers (Kersten 2010). However, principals typically gravitate to a smaller, close-knit group of district administrative colleagues to whom they can turn for support. Superintendents, on the other hand, may feel more isolated, that is, without close district peers. If they work in a large enough school district, they may cultivate some collegial relationships with other central office administrators, but even these are not completely peer based. Talking with a central office colleague is not the same as turning to another superintendent for support and counsel.

As a novice superintendent, you must adjust to a certain level of district isolation and loneliness. You must accept the fact that others will interact with you on a less personal level. To succeed, you need a high level of self-confidence to compensate for a lack of close personal relationships in the district.

SUMMARY

Assessing your personal fit for the superintendency is an important first step in seeking the position. This chapter has explored the uniqueness of the position. Discussed were the challenges superintendents must be prepared to face, as well as how successful superintendents thrive on the challenges of the position. You will want to consider these important points when assessing whether the superintendency is for you.

TWO

Looking Before You Leap

Consider for a moment just how few superintendencies are available nationwide given that there are only 13,934 school districts in the country (The National Center for Educational Statistics 2009). Such a low number makes the superintendency one of the most select and sought-after administrative positions in public education. Anyone appointed to the position of superintendent of schools can take great pride knowing that a school community has enough confidence to select them for such an important leadership position.

Yet, as personally satisfying as this may seem, aspiring superintendents must guard against letting their egos drive their job searches. They must take a step back and objectively assess their fit for a particular position; otherwise, they can find themselves in a superintendency for which they are not a good match. A poor career move at the superintendent level could prove detrimental to their chances for future success.

Consider how you felt when you were appointed to your first administrative position. If you are similar to most administrators, you experienced the euphoria of success. You took satisfaction in knowing that you came out on top of what was most likely a complex search process.

Soon, though, you also experienced reality. The "honeymoon" was probably short lived. The initial thrill of selection soon gave way to the demands of the position. In fact, you may have found within as little as a few months that your "approval rating," much like that of any U.S. president, had declined. As you exerted your leadership and made some difficult decisions, you soon realized how hard it was to be perpetually popular.

As you consider your first superintendency, be aware that you will very likely move through the honeymoon stage rather quickly. As you do, you will discover just how important it is to be in a position that is a

9

good match for your skill set. One way to increase your chances of landing in such a position is to do your homework. That is, research the district and position before making application and continuing throughout the selection process.

DETERMINING YOUR MATCH

To avoid the "ego trap," which means accepting a superintendency just because it is offered, you must actively research every position before deciding to apply. You cannot assume that you will automatically succeed in the superintendency because of your past administrative success. Remember that almost all individuals who rise to the superintendency do so because they were successful at multiple, lower administrative levels.

Unfortunately, similar to the warnings you receive when you make a mutual fund investment, prior performance is no guarantee of future success in a superintendency. Some very skilled and highly competent superintendents have failed in certain school districts. While most found positions elsewhere, others left the profession on a sour note (Polka and Litchka 2008).

It is important to recognize that boards of education, district employees, and community members are much more likely to "turn" on the superintendent than other administrators. Principals can isolate themselves to some degree from unfair treatment by building local constituencies. Superintendents, especially those relatively new to a district, do not enjoy this luxury. Most stakeholders do not have the opportunity to get to know them on the same personal level that they do their principals. These less personal relationships can work against the success of superintendents.

To a large extent, superintendents can be compared to baseball managers. For every Bobby Cox, who managed the Atlanta Braves successfully for decades, many more are "out" in five years or less. When controversies emerge, it is easy to blame the superintendent, whose political support is often limited.

To increase your chances of ensuring that you are a good fit for a position, the first step is to do your homework. By taking your ego out of the job search equation and evaluating each opening dispassionately, you can increase your chances for long-term success.

STRATEGIES FOR DOING YOUR HOMEWORK

Before even applying for a position, begin by utilizing a variety of strategies to develop a solid understanding of the school district.

Strategy 1: Be Active Outside Your School District

Perhaps the best way to "get to know" a school district is to observe it from a variety of perspectives. You must avoid becoming district bound. Some aspiring superintendents tend to focus almost exclusively on their current position. They immerse themselves in their own school districts and rarely reach outside. If you are considering the superintendency, you must find a balance between professional activities in and out of your district.

This, though, means that you will have to decide how to balance your district responsibilities against outside activities. You do not want to lose sight of the reality that being out of district too much can be detrimental to your career. However, if you find the correct balance, you can use involvement in local and state professional and community organizations to gather information about school districts to which you might apply. Through these informal contacts, you can learn a great deal about school district superintendencies in your area.

Strategy 2: Start Cultivating a Personal Professional Network

Education is a people-centered business (Kersten 2010b). Because school districts are so people focused, it is relatively simple to learn a great deal of information about any school district if you so choose.

The more extensive your personal network, the greater the likelihood that you can develop a comprehensive, realistic understanding of any school district before you even apply. How often have you heard of an administrator who accepted a superintendency only to find out later that two or three board members were leaving soon? Similarly, have you known a superintendent who accepted a position only to discover that the district was in dire financial straits and facing severe program reductions?

One way to avoid these surprises is to build a broad personal network. Time-tested ways to accomplish this include:

- Attending local professional meetings regularly;
- Volunteering to serve as a representative on local boards such as the special education cooperative;
- Seeking out community service boards and volunteering to participate in activities;
- Initiating contacts with other administrators in your area. Be the one who calls your neighboring administrators to discuss issues or to ask for advice; and
- Looking for opportunities to be a social network leader. Consider scheduling informal breakfast or lunch get-togethers. Organize outside social events such as a golf outing, a day at a spa, or a trip to a sporting event. Be inclusive rather than exclusive.

When others get to know you on a personal level, they are more likely to share their real thoughts. If all your personal interactions are superficial, you cannot expect others to be frank.

Strategy 3: Read, Read, Read

Although you can learn a great deal about a particular position through personal contacts, you should not ignore other sources of information. As access to data has expanded, you have unprecedented opportunities to research almost any superintendency from the comfort of your home. There is a wealth of information available through a variety of resources on the Internet.

With a few clicks of the mouse, you can easily find a school district's website or read local articles chronicling recent events in the district. Also, you can access statewide databases for information on district finances, student achievement, and teacher education and experience.

Strategy 4: Utilize Nontraditional Sources for Information

In addition to the strategies above, do not overlook nontraditional sources of information. A relatively new source for gathering information about the district and especially members of the school board is to "Google" them. Similarly, social networking sites such as LinkedIn and Facebook may provide fresh perspectives not available elsewhere. You can be assured that search consultants and school board members will check on you through each of these.

If you do not live in the area, a vacation or quick weekend trip can be enlightening. You may want to contact area realtor offices and ask for their perspectives on school districts in the area. Real estate agent evaluations often reflect the sentiment in the community.

The more you know about a school district and especially the superintendency, the better informed you will be. Once you have done your homework, you will have learned a great deal about the school district, as well as the superintendent opening. You will have completed the first step in determining your match for the position.

EXTENDING YOUR "FIT" ASSESSMENT

After you have established your initial fit, your work is only partially complete. If you apply and are invited into the interview process, here is where the real match process begins. Before you interview, you should take some time to clarify for yourself your core values. Ask yourself what would be most important for you to accept the position? What type of school district culture do you value? Be true to your beliefs. You must recognize that the employment decision is a two-way street. You must resist the temptation to be mesmerized by a desire to find your first superintendency.

Although your initial research may have indicated that the position was a good match, remember that many unknown factors lurk. An all-important next step begins the minute you receive a call from the search consultant inviting you to interview.

Those who are too anxious to be a superintendent or are very ego driven may only focus on "selling" themselves rather than objectively assessing the position. If the superintendency you accept ultimately proves a poor match, this one decision may be a career ender. What is more important is to use the school district selection process as a barometer of "fit."

Taking Your First "Reading"

As you enter the interview process, it is helpful to understand the primary motivation of search consultants. Since they have invited you for a screening interview, in essence, you have already made the "cut." If this is your first time meeting representatives of a particular search firm, it is possible that they are interviewing you to help them decide if you may be a good candidate for other searches in addition to the one for which they called you. If they already know you, they probably already have a good sense of you who are.

Search firms must produce candidates. They must present a full candidate slate to the board of education. This means that they are probably less concerned about your personal success than ensuring that the boards have sufficient candidates to consider. Many search firms operate under the unwritten belief that their role is to provide the board of education with an array of candidates who they consider qualified. It is up to the board of education to assess the fit and make the selection.

As such, you cannot expect to get a completely accurate picture of the district's situation from search consultants. The consultants are there to create excitement about the position. As a result, they will tend to minimize any problems and accentuate the positives. To get beyond the generic assessment, you need to be prepared to ask questions. Here are several to consider.

- How long has the current superintendent been in the position and why is the superintendent leaving?
- What are the backgrounds of the board members and how long have they been on the board?
- Are any board members expected to leave in the near future?
- How well do board members work together?
- During the past few years, what major challenges has the district faced and what challenges are anticipated over the next few years?
- What are the district priorities for the next two to three years?

- Based on the district's financial projections, what is its five-year financial outlook?
- What is the history of collective bargaining in the district?
- What is the relationship between the school board and teachers?
- How well do administrators work together?
- What are the expectations of the board members for the superintendent?

The answers to these questions will provide you with a more detailed picture of the school district and the position.

In addition to the interview, the consultants will usually present you with a series of school district documents such as a community profile and financial reports. Although it is important to study these materials yourself, you would be well served to ask administrative colleagues such as your current superintendent and business manager to review them also. Because of their experience and knowledge, they may note important information you might otherwise not consider.

District Interview Process

If, after the screening process, you are asked back for additional interviews, you will have ample opportunities to get to know the district well. The superintendent interview process typically includes multiple levels. You can expect to be interviewed by a variety of stakeholders, often as part of a very long and intense day. You want to view this process as an opportunity rather than an obstacle to overcome.

It is during this phase of the process that you must be especially judgmental. You have to force yourself to remain as objective as possible and avoid being swayed by the lure of success. As you move from one interview group to another, use your time with each to help you decide whether you are in sync with the district. As the day unfolds, see if you become more or less excited about the position. If you are honest with yourself, these interviews can be a powerful barometer of fit.

You must be ready to pull out of the search if you do not feel a connection. As you meet with board members, teachers, parents, and other community members, you have to ask yourself if you could see yourself working well in this environment before you make a decision.

One effective technique you can use to assess your comfort level with the school board is to understand their expectations for you. A way to accomplish this is to provide each board member with three index cards during your interview. Ask them to write down one personal expectation they would have for you on each card. You can gain valuable insights to help you decide whether the position is a good fit. If employed, you will also know each board member's priorities.

You also should consider identifying a colleague on whom you could "bounce off" your feelings about the position. The conversation may be just the type of process you need to help you make a more objective assessment of fit.

Yes, you may worry about how the search consultants will view you if you decide to pull out of the search. Some may initially express disappointment with you. Even so, you must accept this reality. Ultimately, if you are direct in explaining your decision, most will respect you. Be direct about your decision. For example, you might tell them that, after spending a full day in the district, you did not see yourself as a good fit.

At the same time, be careful not to postpone your decision until you receive the offer. If you know the position is not right for you, as a professional, you should drop out of the search before the selection is made. By completing your job search due diligence, you can take comfort in knowing that, if you accept a position, you have increased the likelihood of your success.

SUMMARY

Deciding whether a particular superintendency is a good career move begins with focused research on both the position and the school district. This chapter has discussed ways you can dispassionately assess your fit for a particular position. Offered also were strategies you could use to "do your homework," including successfully navigating the selection process.

THREE

Getting Off to a Successful Start

As everyone knows, first impressions can be critical to success. As a new superintendent, initial impressions others form about you will certainly impact how you are perceived and ultimately your overall success. As a result, it is imperative to make the most of your first contacts with everyone associated with the school district. Remember that no matter how extensive the superintendent selection process, most stakeholders will still not know you very well. In fact, some may feel anxiety about the leadership change. These feelings may be the result of poor experiences with new administrators in the past who interviewed well but never lived up to expectations.

The day you walk into your superintendency, all eyes will be focused on you. What most people want to know is who you really are. You can be assured that everyone's personal antennas will be up. However, if your performance exceeds expectations, you will soon begin to build your support base. Below are suggestions to help you make a positive first impression in the school district as well as during your first school board meeting.

ESTABLISHING YOUR IMAGE

It is important to recognize that, while you cannot ensure your long-term success as superintendent in your first two months, you could easily scuttle it. People tend to be judgmental and place great weight on their first impressions. Some will access their personal networks to find out more about you. Teachers may contact teachers in your former district to "check you out." Parents may know someone who had previous interactions with you. Whether what they discover is accurate or not, they will

17

filter their initial impressions through these lenses. Consequently, how you interact with them during your first couple of months will either confirm or refute their initial judgments.

As you step into the superintendency, you should formulate a plan to build the personal image you want to project. Below are several image-building strategies you may want to consider.

Strategy 1: Be Genuine

Have you ever worked with administrators who projected artificial-ity? These are individuals who are already looking over your shoulder to see who else is in the room as they are talking to you. They tend to be people who even though they met you several times never seem to know or remember much about you. They seem to ask you the same personal questions every time they see you. Often they appear outwardly friendly; however, you never really get to know them.

People often see through these personality types. Yet, as long as they do nothing to negatively impact someone, they are often tolerated. How-ever, is being tolerated sufficient, especially for long-term success? What is more crucial to superintendents' success, particularly at the point that they must deliver bad news, is the level of respect they have earned from others. If stakeholders perceive the superintendent as someone who is "real," they are more likely to hear and trust what is said.

Achieving a reputation as someone who is genuine requires a commit-ment of time, often when time is at a premium. However, earning this reputation and the trust that accompanies it can help you build long-term support. Here are several ways to send the message that you are a genu-ine person.

- Get to know, if at all possible, every employee's name. In large school districts, this may not be possible. However, the more peo-ple you know on a first name basis the better. One way to accom-plish this is to find yearbooks and/or other employee photos. Before you are scheduled to meet with any group or visit one of the schools, review the names and photos. However, when you first meet them, do not pretend to know them. This will appear overly familiar. Rather, introduce yourself and begin making a connection.
- Make a point of sitting in on as many meetings as you can during your first summer. Curriculum committees and professional devel-opment sessions bring teachers and administrators together. Listen-ing rather than talking should be your focus. By attending these, you can improve your people recognition skills even if this is not normally one of your strengths.
- Visit summer school classes, using the time to connect with stu-dents and teachers.

- Walk through the central office, regularly dropping into offices and greeting people in the halls. This shows that you value personal contact while sending the message that you are an accessible, open leader.
- Make a point of joining the central office and school staffs during breaks or lunch hours. Not only will they get to know you in an informal setting, but this will help you get to know them better as well.

Strategy 2: Focus on Being a Learner First

Superintendents tend to be "take charge" leaders. However, they must guard against being too assertive when they are new to a position. As you move into the superintendency, you should resist the urge to overparticipate, which may be interpreted as controlling. Rather, view your first three months on the job as an opportunity to be a learner. No one will criticize you for moving cautiously. However, they may question your style of leadership if you start making too many changes too soon.

Strategy 3: Get to Know and Understand the Perspectives of Individual School Board Members

Shortly after you settle into your office, you should invite each school board member to sit down for an informal chat. This is an excellent way to begin to get to know them on a personal level. It is appropriate to use this time to tell them about your family and learn about theirs. It is important for them to connect with you as a person, not just a district administrator. In addition, these sessions will allow you to develop an understanding of their priorities and expectations for both you and the district.

Ideally, your chats should be conducted at the district office where board members see you in your leadership role. In preparation for the visits, leave "no stone unturned." This means ensuring that the office staff knows board members are visiting and are ready to greet them enthusiastically. Find a comfortable meeting spot, preferably in your office. Make a point of clearing any clutter and presenting a highly organized business look. Insist on no interruptions. This will send the message that the board members' time and thoughts are your priority.

Although these sessions are informal in nature, they should be well structured and focused. It is helpful to prepare a series of questions such as those below which you can use to guide the discussion.

- Why did you decide to become a board member?
- What do you view as the strengths of the school district?
- What have been some of the primary district priorities since you joined the board?

- Do you have a particular interest or focus as a board member?
- What should the district continue to do?
- What should the district stop doing?
- What should the district consider doing?

As you meet, focus on listening and note taking. However, make sure that your note taking is not excessive. Otherwise, you will lose the feeling of a conversation. This is not a time to lobby a point of view or attempt to show how knowledgeable you are on any topic. You want board members to leave feeling that they had an opportunity to get to know you and that you heard what they said.

Strategy 4: Begin Establishing Relationships with Your Administrative Team Members

No single group of individuals is more important to your success than your administrative team. The size of the team will, of course, vary depending upon your school district. Whether you have one or fifty colleagues, you should begin connecting with your administrators early. Plan to meet individually with each of them.

A good approach to begin getting to know them is to meet with them on their "turf." Ask them to walk you through their school. Encourage them to show you what is important to them, not what you want to see.

Similar to other employee groups, they, too, will worry about their potential relationship with you. When you meet, invite them to share their perspectives on every aspect of the district. They have information about the district no one else does. It is your responsibility to make them feel welcome and comfortable. If you are friendly, open, and encouraging, you will set a positive first tone. As with other groups, ask questions, take notes, and listen well.

Strategy 5: Meet and Greet

An initial critical mistake superintendents can make is becoming office bound. When you move into the superintendency, your self-survival skills kick in. You feel that you have to know everything about everything. This mentality can isolate you from people who want to know you personally. If you are not careful, you could easily get a reputation as someone not in touch with the district.

Although there are some essential management tasks that you must tackle, you want to think about relationship building first. This means that you should identify as many possible people and groups to meet and greet. When you were a principal, you did this by focusing on school-level employees, key parents, some students, other administrators, and certain district staff. Now, as superintendent, you must broaden your contact circle.

One way to accomplish this is to create a list of key contacts. These should include but not be limited to the following:

- Leaders of school-supported parent organizations, such as PTOs and booster clubs;
- Police, park, and village officials;
- Local newspaper reporters; and
- Other area superintendents.

You may also want to seek out key leaders of community service organizations and possibly the local Chamber of Commerce. However, before deciding to join any group, consider the political consequences of selecting one over another. Remember that your time will be quite limited once the school year begins. Also, do not assume that you must join an organization. In some communities or school districts, membership is a superintendent expectation. In others, it is viewed as a personal option. If you are unsure, ask the former superintendent, board president, or other administrators to advise you.

Finally, do not forget to contact your local teacher and support staff union/association representatives. Relationships that exist between the employee groups and the district administration and school board are quite distinct among school districts. In some instances, these are grounded in collective bargaining agreements. In others, the relationships can be informal.

Before you schedule meetings with these leaders, you should do some research to ensure that you understand any legal requirements in your state. Also, try and find out as much as you can about the existing relationships between employee groups and the school board/administration. Resist the temptation to form prejudgments about the groups or their leaders. This will help you avoid any initial missteps.

As a new superintendent, you have an opportunity to begin a fresh relationship. It is in your best interest to approach these group leaders as you would others. By being friendly and focusing on listening, you increase your chances of "getting off on the right foot."

AVOID THE UNKNOWN

It is not uncommon for superintendents, who are new to their school districts, to fall into an unexpected trap. A parent, teacher, or other staff member, as part of a casual conversation, may ask what appears to be an innocent question. For example, someone might ask you what you believe is the most effective gifted education model. Without thinking much about it, you may offer an opinion. Unfortunately, you do not know that this is a district hot button issue. Within an hour, your opinion may be a topic of discussion in the schools or around the community.

As a beginning superintendent, you want to avoid inadvertently taking sides on issues. Rather, when asked for your opinion, it is good practice to turn the question back to the person first. By asking them to explain why they are asking, you may be able to develop a sense of potential district controversy.

You should avoid becoming embroiled in issues before you have had a chance to do any fact-finding. It is always safer to say that you would rather not express an opinion on a topic until you have time to study it. For example, if a parent asks for your opinion on the gifted program, you could comment that you value the needs of all students. However, you could add that you need more time to learn about it. The next step is especially important. Tell the person that you will get back to him/her. Then, make sure you do.

GETTING TO KNOW DISTRICT OPERATIONAL SERVICES

Some beginning superintendents focus exclusively on people and programs. These are indeed critical for new superintendents. Yet, effectiveness of instruction is impacted by operational services such as facilities, transportation, and food services. The summer is an excellent time to become familiar with each.

By familiarizing yourself with school sites and other district facilities, you can quickly gauge the condition of each and even identify needed improvements. You might find safety hazards, which you can correct before problems develop.

If you are in a district large enough to have a director of building and grounds, this person can be your tour guide. An added benefit of a director-led tour is that this administrator knows all the custodial and maintenance personnel and can introduce you. These site visits allow you to establish a first contact with these key support staff members while developing a good feel for district facilities.

Just as important are transportation and food services. If these operate smoothly and efficiently, you will be able to free up time to focus on other transition activities. Since you are an experienced administrator, you can probably gauge the effectiveness of each. Similar to the approach you used with facilities, build time into your schedule to tour facilities and meet with available personnel. In addition to relying on your own judgment, you should ask your administrators for their assessment of each. They can alert you to potential issues.

PREPARING FOR YOUR FIRST BOARD MEETING

One of the first hurdles new superintendents must jump is conducting their first school board meeting. You may have attended many as an observer during your career. Now, you will find yourself on center stage. For some board members, this will be the primary way they interact with you. As a result, your performance as superintendent may be judged to a large extent by board member perceptions of you in this venue.

Unfortunately, school board members are usually not present when you do much of your most important work. They rarely see you directly solving day-to-day district problems, setting high expectations with employees, or leading well-run, in-district meetings. They probably are not there when you stand by a tough but important decision with employees or special interest groups. But, they do see you for a few hours each month at school board meetings.

A common fear of beginning superintendents is that their school board meetings may be unfocused and controversial. They worry that questions will be asked that they cannot answer or that they will fumble their responses. Most new superintendents hope that they will inherit board members who work together as a team and refrain from competitive behavior.

When you begin to feel the tensions associated with your first board meeting, remember that your worst fears are rarely realized. The mind, when faced with uncertainty and fear of the unknown, tends to focus on the worst case scenario. This is a good time to remember that you were hired because others had confidence in you.

One way to allay some of your fears is to overprepare for your first meeting. The more prepared you feel, the more likely it is that you will present yourself as self-assured. At the same time, you must avoid the trap of overinvolvement. Be prepared to respond only to those items to which you would reasonably be expected to contribute.

Since your first board meeting is likely within your initial two or three weeks on the job, you should begin planning for it before you even assume your position. The three- or four-month timeframe from appointment to your official beginning allows you time to do your homework.

Here are several ways to use this transition period to help ensure that your initial board meeting is productive and uneventful.

- As soon as you are appointed, contact the current superintendent or, if appropriate, the superintendent's secretary and request copies of key district documents. These should include board books/packets and minutes from the past year, minutes from recent district administrative staff meetings, and written communications from the superintendent to the board. You can study these to better understand the structure of meetings, as well as the roles administrators play. You will also be able to develop some sense of the actual board discussion.

- Attend a school board meeting as an observer. In all likelihood, you will be invited to the meeting at which you are appointed. You should stay for the entire session, using the time to observe the administrators and board members and observe how board meetings are typically conducted.
- Schedule meetings with both the current superintendent and school board president to discuss how board agendas are prepared. Find out if you are expected to have the board president approve the final agenda. Do not be afraid to probe them to understand past expectations for communication between the superintendent and the board members, especially the president.
- As a new superintendent, always focus on honoring past processes. Avoid making any changes in board meeting procedures too soon. You will be in a much better position to make any necessary changes in a few months.
- Seek out the superintendent's secretary for assistance. The coordination of the board book/packet process is usually assigned to the superintendent's secretary or higher-level clerical staff members. They generally have a wealth of both formal and informal information. They maintain extensive files of key documents and oversee the board book production schedule. Many are willing to offer their advice. If asked, they may even share information or insights that others cannot.
- Determine preexisting expectations for administrators and other employees to attend board meetings. This way, you will know who you can expect to respond to questions as needed during the meeting.
- Probe policies related to audience participation. Laws that govern audience participation at school board meetings vary from state to state. So do local district guidelines. Understanding these beforehand will help you avoid potential on-the-spot confusion should an audience member ask to speak.
- If board meetings are televised, view these as opportunities to learn a great deal without actually attending the meetings.
- Try to identify another area superintendent who is well respected and willing to share advice about board meetings and school board relationship building. The superintendent will be flattered that you sought his or her assistance. Also, your due diligence will either confirm or correct information you already gathered from other sources about successful board meetings. Best yet, you will have found a potential mentor!

Once you complete your upfront research and assume your position, you should focus directly on preparations for your first meeting. Above all, think organization. Your goal is to prepare the most organized, mistake-free board packet possible. Also, you want to ensure it arrives in board member hands promptly. This will send the message that you are a detail-oriented, well-organized superintendent.

To accomplish this, you will need to oversee the process personally while allowing others to do what they are expected to do. Begin by establishing a board packet timeline. Since you do not know your staff well yet, it is essential to build in extra time for each step. Even the most experienced superintendents periodically find themselves stretched for time when something unexpected occurs. It is always better to finish your board packet a day early rather than find yourself distributing it to board member homes late.

Here are some tips to consider as you prepare for your first board meeting.

- Develop a board meeting agenda template that includes cyclical items. This way you will have the basic headings listed and only need to add details each month.
- Create a month-by-month list of reoccurring monthly agenda items. In addition, incorporate planned key reports into the appropriate month. Enlist the assistance of office staff and central office administrators to suggest items to include as well as to review the accuracy of the list. After it is complete, you may want to invite your mentor superintendent to critique it.
- Clarify the roles and responsibilities of office staff and administrators in the preparation of written reports as well as the assembly and distribution of the board book.
- Proofread, proofread, and proofread. If you are similar to many people, you tend to read over typos and missing words. To tighten up the final product, identify at least two other people to proofread every document in the board book at various points in the development process. This will help minimize mistakes that board members may interpret as lack of thoroughness.
- Verify legal requirements for posting and distributing board meeting notices. Although someone is probably responsible for ensuring compliance, failure to meet requirements can lead to unnecessary controversy.
- Review the board room meeting setup. In the spirit of thoroughness, it is prudent to double-check the board room arrangement. Make sure that audience materials are accessible and all technology is operational.

You may rely on others for many of these items as you become comfortable with their skills. However, you would be wise to verify these key details firsthand during your first few months on the job.

CONTACT YOUR AMERICAN ASSOCIATION OF SCHOOL ADMINISTRATORS (AASA) LOCAL AFFILIATE

In addition to the excellent resources offered from AASA, state affiliates are an invaluable resource to new superintendents. You can count on them to represent you and your professional interests. Many offer beginning superintendent workshops, mentoring programs, legal counsel, and informational materials. As part of your transition plan, you should contact your state affiliate to learn more about available assistance.

SUMMARY

Chapter 3 has explored ways to help make your first couple of months as superintendent as productive as possible. The first section focused on how to project the type of personal image you want. Several strategies were suggested to build relationships with a variety of stakeholders both within and outside the school district. Also discussed was the importance of familiarizing yourself with school district operational and support programs. How to prepare for and conduct a well-organized first school board meeting was also examined. Many ideas were offered to help you make full use of available planning time. Also discussed were specific suggestions to enhance the success of your first board meeting.

FOUR

Establishing Your Leadership

For decades, school boards primarily expected superintendents to be sound school district managers. If they "ran a tight ship," that is, kept a close eye on the budget, ensured smooth school operations, and led the teacher contract negotiation process, they were generally successful. Instructional leadership was considered primarily the responsibility of assistant superintendents for instruction and building-level administrators.

In recent years, expectations for superintendent performance have shifted. So much more is expected of superintendents today, and even more will be in the future. As critics have questioned the efficacy of public education, calls for superintendents to be educational leaders have grown (Hunt, Watkins, Kersten, and Tripses 2011) . School boards today want superintendents who have the knowledge and skills necessary to increase student achievement, manage finances, and lead district improvement efforts.

This leadership emphasis is clearly reflected in the ways school boards select their superintendents. Consider for a moment the complex and sophisticated selection processes that superintendent candidates face in most school districts. Candidates must survive multiple interviews with search consultants and school board members. They also face one interview after another with an array of teachers, parents, and community members.

What also has changed about this process in recent years is the focus of the interviews themselves. Yes, everyone still wants a superintendent who knows how to manage the school district efficiently and effectively. That is a given. However, they also want someone who demonstrates instructional leadership skills. Boards of education seek superintendents who they believe will improve their district schools while increasing student achievement. They expect them during the interview process to present concrete ideas. Also, they expect them to explain how they will document results.

This focused emphasis is somewhat different from what you may have experienced at some point in your career. Do you remember working in a school district where it was acceptable for the superintendent to present board goals, such as these, to the school board?

- To prepare our students to be productive students in a democratic society.
- To develop life-long learners.
- To educate our students to compete successfully in the complex, diverse world of the twenty-first century.

On the surface, who could argue that these lofty ideals are not worthwhile? In fact, in the past, board members generally found these acceptable. They may not have even raised questions about their specificity. Just presenting district goals was itself sufficient. Unfortunately, these types of goals had little or no impact on school improvement or student achievement. After presentation to the board, they resided in documents on bookshelves. They were reviewed only when someone asked to see a copy of the district goals.

As demands for increased accountability have grown, so, too, has the oversight function of school boards. The days of presenting generic, altruistic goals are long gone. Superintendents today must understand how to improve schools and increase student achievement.

SUPERINTENDENT LEADERSHIP RESEARCH

Until relatively recently, little sound research was available on the role of superintendents in increasing student achievement. However, two prominent researchers, Marzano and Waters (2009), have begun to unravel what it is that successful superintendents do to increase student achievement. Through their research, Marzano and Waters (2009) identified several major findings related to the superintendent's role in influencing student achievement. As a beginning school district leader, this is important information to consider.

Superintendents Make a Difference

If you ask educational stakeholders whether they believe superintendents make a positive difference in their local school districts, almost always the answer is yes. Intuitively, people believe that superintendents are important to school district success. However, these responses often emanate from personal opinions rather than actual research.

Now emerging is new evidence documenting the critical importance of effective district leadership, especially related to student achievement gains. Marzano and Waters (2009, 5) note "that when district leaders are carrying out their leadership responsibilities effectively, student achievement across the district is positively affected." Successful superintendents are truly difference makers!

As part of their analysis, Marzano and Waters (2009) pinpointed five specific superintendent leadership behaviors associated with increased student achievement.

Behavior 1: Ensuring Collaborative Goal Setting

Marzano and Waters point out that successful superintendents include all relevant stakeholders in the establishment of nonnegotiable district goals. Principals and those who are responsible for implementing district goals must be highly involved. Furthermore, for the improvement process to succeed, those included must agree to support the accomplishment of the goals. As a consequence, superintendents who get results are more inclusive rather than less inclusive.

Behavior 2: Establishing Nonnegotiable Goals for Achievement and Instruction

Even though establishing collaborative goals is important, if they become negotiable, little is achieved. Successful superintendents ensure the establishment of nonnegotiable goals for achievement and instruction. All staff members, administrators, board members, and teachers are expected to make student achievement a priority. Action plans, which include specific achievement targets, are written for the district and building levels as well as for specific subpopulations of students.

Richard DuFour (2007) captures the concept of nonnegotiability in his discussion of his top-down leadership theory. He uses the terms "tight" and "loose" when describing the school leader expectations. He argues that effective leaders must, at times, be "tight" or unbending about their priorities. That is, there are times when you must demand that something be done. This does not mean being an authoritarian leader but, rather, firm on expectations. His theory applies well to district leadership. If you want to be a strong educational leader, you must remain "tight" about the importance of focusing on student achievement.

DuFour also notes that leaders, in some instances, should be "loose." Marzano and Waters (2009) note that superintendents should allow others the autonomy to help craft action plans. They should permit them some flexibility to decide how best to deliver the curriculum. While the district establishes a broad-based, common classroom instructional design framework all must follow, superintendents should be "loose" about specific teaching methodologies.

Marzano and Waters (2009) also speak about the importance of superintendents expecting principals to lead the achievement of nonnegotiable goals. As superintendent, you must expect that your principals are far more than passive participants in achieving district achievement goals. In addition, you must never permit them to do anything that undermines district efforts. This means setting high and clear performance expectations for principals. For example, superintendents must expect that their principals have a plan to hold teachers accountable for their students' achievement.

Behavior 3: Creating Board Alignment With and Support of District Goals

Effective superintendents work with the school boards to ensure that board members maintain a primary focus on student achievement. As a result, other priorities are not allowed to distract from district-wide improvement efforts, including through the diversion of needed resources. As superintendent, you will need to work with your board to solidify goals through the adoption of a multiyear improvement plan. You will also need to help school boards maintain their focus on student achievement and not get distracted by their personal agendas.

Behavior 4: Maintaining a Focus on Achievement and Instructional Goals

An essential superintendent responsibility is leading efforts to continuously monitor both student achievement and instructional goals. This includes requiring that each school remains focused on its school-level plan. As superintendent, you must expect your principals to monitor teacher agreed-upon plans and regularly observe classroom instruction. Principals need to meet with faculty members regularly to analyze student achievement data. They should also demonstrate how they have taken corrective actions with teachers as warranted.

Behavior 5: Ensuring that Resources Are Allocated to Support Achievement and Instructional Goals

School districts are often fraught with one new initiative after another. These can dilute the school district's focus on student achievement. As superintendent, you must constantly reinforce the focus on student achievement. At the same time, you need to ensure that adequate resources including personnel, money, time, and materials are provided.

When allocating resources, Marzano and Waters (2009) point out that you need to invest in professional development focused on teachers' and principals' goals. Accordingly, sufficient resources should be directed at professional development aligned with school and district goals. Otherwise, you will hamper your success.

Defined Autonomy

In addition to identifying superintendent behaviors linked to increased achievement, Marzano and Waters (2009) identify one other important finding. They termed it *defined autonomy*. "Defined autonomy means that the superintendent expects building principals and all other administrators in the district to lead within the boundaries defined by district goals" (8). That is, they need to focus their efforts toward the achievement of district goals, especially related to student achievement.

Rather than prescribing and regulating how principals should address district student achievement goals, effective superintendents are tight about their expectations for principals. They require principals to focus on district goals. At the same time, they allow them flexibility to determine how to best accomplish them in their schools.

LEADERSHIP STRATEGIES

Knowing what successful superintendents do to lead their school districts and especially to increase student achievement is important. However, what is equally important for you as a beginning superintendent is to begin to establish your leadership. This is especially important during the first few months in your position when others are forming impressions of you. Discussed below are suggestions you may want to consider as you think about establishing your district leadership.

Focus Exclusively on Your New School District

Have you ever worked in a school district where a new administrator said, "In my last school district, we did it . . ."? This is a sure way to create a barrier between yourself and others while undermining your leadership. A better approach is to broaden the context. For example, instead of saying, "I have had success with this in past districts," you might respond, "I know that some districts have had success with this."

You probably have had many valuable experiences up to this point in your career. In fact, your successes actually provided you with the wealth of knowledge needed to stand out from other candidates during the superintendent search. However, now is the time to begin to align yourself exclusively with your new school district. Avoid references to past districts while utilizing your experiences to lead your new one.

Remember That Pleasing Is Not Leading

Another mistake novice superintendents make is focusing on pleasing others. Some mistakenly believe that, if they keep people happy, they enhance their district leadership. If your goal is to please everyone, you will soon fail. No matter how hard you try, you cannot make everyone happy.

Successful superintendents understand that respected leaders do not focus on pleasing others, including school board members. Rather, they work on earning their respect. As such, they concern themselves with making thoughtful, student-centered decisions whenever possible. If you do, you too will discover that others will respect you even more as a leader. You want to be actively engaged in decision-making even if it means disagreeing at times.

Remember, if you focus on pleasing others, you run the risk of appearing directionless. This will weaken your leadership over time. A key to your success is establishing relationships with stakeholders while remaining true to your ideals. By articulating a consistent message and not shying away from expressing positions on issues, you show others that you are the district leader.

Be Decisive

Few things are more frustrating for school district employees than an indecisive superintendent. In fact, most employees want to work for district leaders who are not afraid to make decisions, even if they do not always agree with them. Without decisive executive leadership, school districts can lose focus and seem rudderless.

Indecisiveness is usually associated with insecurity. Some new superintendents find themselves worrying too much about making unpopular decisions that may lead to controversy. As a result, they often find themselves procrastinating or becoming overly reliant on others to make decisions for them. This does not mean that they should make uninformed decisions. Rather, it is recognizing how timely and thoughtful decision-making contributes to their success.

As a beginning superintendent, it is important to find a balance between over- and underconfidence. However, when in doubt, it is preferable to err on the side of proactive rather than indecisive leadership.

Avoid Overcontrolling Behavior

While indecisive leadership hampers a superintendent's effectiveness, overcontrolling behavior can have a similar impact. Superintendents who feel they must control almost every decision actually limit their effectiveness. Avoid the temptation to lead through control. To appreciate this, consider the following.

Have you ever worked for a superintendent who rarely delegated authority and had to approve even building operational decisions? Under this type of leadership, both administrators and teachers feel powerless. For example, if a superintendent does not allow principals the authority to structure graduation programs or make employment decisions, how invested will they be? Under such leadership, after a relatively short period of time, most employees become less creative and feel unengaged.

If you want to be an effective leader, you should begin by establishing clear lines of authority. Within these lines, you must differentiate between what decisions you will make, such as establishing school improvement and student achievement goals. At the same time, you must be secure enough to permit administrators and other district personnel to make decisions at their respective levels. Even though they may, at times, make some poor decisions, overall you will accomplish more. More importantly, you will create a district culture of shared leadership that will be more likely to earn the trust and support of others.

Do Not Arrive with a Predetermined Agenda

Another mistake some new superintendents make is announcing a district improvement agenda almost immediately after they arrive. As you transition to the superintendency, you may have already formed some perceptions about district needs. You may even see several areas prime for improvement.

In some circumstances, you may even have been given "marching orders" by the board. If you have, be transparent about them, especially with your administrative team. You might ask them their thoughts on how to address them collectively.

Even so, it is most often wise to avoid making any substantial changes before taking your time to get to know the district. Do not feel pressured by board members to act too quickly. You will find that you have sufficient time to study the district and understand the culture. After you do, you will be in a stronger position to make informed recommendations.

Avoid Favoritism

The most effective leaders are perceived by others as fair. That is, they treat others equally. As a new superintendent, you must avoid the temptation to favor certain administrators or board members. Otherwise, you can easily undermine your leadership success.

On a personal and even professional level, you may feel more connected with one individual or another. However, you would be well served to avoid any public display of favoritism. If others perceive that you cater to favorites, jealousies will develop. Others will be less likely to follow your lead.

Take "I" Out of Your Vocabulary

Have you ever watched NASCAR drivers interviewed following their victories? Do you notice how they answer every question with "we"? This does not mean that you should follow their lead. Rather, what you should recognize from this is the importance of emphasizing team over self.

New superintendents who are egocentric are rarely accepted well by other district personnel. These individuals come across as credit-takers. They want to tell you how they were responsible personally for every district success. Everything centers on them.

If you want to be accepted as the district leader, avoid the "I" syndrome. Find ways to recognize the accomplishments of others. Effective leaders innately know what they have accomplished. Devote more energy to crediting others. Do not be the type of leader who "toots his or her own horn."

SUMMARY

Highly effective superintendents are respected for their strong leadership. This chapter examined research on the role of the superintendent in improving schools and student achievement. Also offered were suggestions on how you, as a beginning superintendent, can establish your leadership early in your tenure in your school district.

FIVE

Working Effectively with the School Board

One of the greatest challenges new superintendents face is working effectively with their school boards. What makes this so unique is that, for the first time in their administrative careers, superintendents find that their job security lies directly in the hands of several elected members of the community. As such, they must recognize that, to enjoy long-term success, they need to earn the support of a majority of their school board members.

Superintendents find this relationship very different from that which they experienced as principals. Previously, their interactions with boards centered primarily on parent organizations, such as PTAs and PTOs, which were only advisory. These parent groups had very little influence on a principal's performance beyond sharing informal perceptions. Principals themselves were evaluated by their superintendents. Even though boards of education, at times, may have crossed this supervisory line, the primary responsibility for the evaluation of administrators still fell to the superintendent.

JOB SECURITY MYTHS

Have you ever had anyone tell you that the average tenure of a superintendent is three years or less? The fact of the matter is that this is inaccurate. Yes, there are some districts that are so dysfunctional that superintendent turnover is common. However, in most districts, superintendents remain in their positions for many years (Kowalski et al. 2010).

A common myth is that superintendents come and go quite regularly. This misconception is one of the primary reasons some very talented

35

administrators sometimes choose to remain at the building or central office levels. They fear for their job security.

Consider for a moment the tenure of superintendents in your area. Have not most been in their positions at least five to seven years? Do almost all who leave do so because of retirement or to accept another position of their choice? This is the more common scenario.

Because the superintendency is such a visible position, perceptions about job stress and insecurity sometimes overshadow reality. In truth, the vast majority of school board members want their superintendents to succeed. Unlike Donald Trump, they do not hire them to fire them. Even though some board members may raise tough questions or even challenge their superintendents publicly, this does not always indicate a lack of support. Rather, it is more likely related to board member perceptions that they must be independent from the administration and fully analyze issues presented to them.

BUILDING POSITIVE RELATIONSHIPS WITH SCHOOL BOARD MEMBERS

Talented, committed district leaders have a high success rate. One of the ways they achieve their success is by focusing from day one on establishing productive relationships with their school board members. Have you ever served on any board? If you have, you can appreciate how board members feel. When they are elected, many automatically assume that they will be very involved in the behind-the-scenes functions of the district. They may expect to be consulted regularly for their opinions.

Unfortunately, new board members are sometimes asked to make decisions on actions without much background information. If elected in the spring, they may even be asked to vote for a district budget with little knowledge of the district's finances. This can be confusing for board members.

Some soon discover that much of the district work happens without their direct involvement. Others see board members leaning heavily on the district administration for direction. Superintendents who fail to recognize the need to prepare board members for their role may see their board relationships deteriorate. Successful superintendents ensure that new and even existing board members are trained on their roles and responsibilities.

This process begins with strong communication between the superintendent and school board members. If board members feel uninformed or believe that their opinions are largely ignored by the administration, they can quickly become disillusioned. This can result in either board member withdrawal or even in aggressive board behavior.

Unless you are told otherwise, you should cultivate a strong working relationship with your board president. In this way, board members have a person to look to for communication with you. The president can also serve as your point person on numerous issues.

As a new superintendent, you have to plan for good communication. You should not believe that just because you are hard working and dedicated that you will automatically have good relationships. Here are some strategies which you should consider to help you establish good working relationships with your school board members.

Strategy 1: Take Time to Understand District Expectations for Superintendent/ Board Relations

When new superintendents arrive, most people anticipate some change. In fact, your board may have hired you precisely because you were different from your predecessor. However, you should not automatically assume that they are looking for a change in communication style.

A good rule of thumb is to maintain the level of communication currently in place until after you have had time to do your homework. This begins with studying any documents that the former superintendent typically sent to board members. Your executive assistant can be an excellent source for documents. He or she can also provide perspectives on how superintendent/board communication was handled in the past. Also, you should take into consideration information you gathered during your selection process. Think about what they asked you. These questions may alert you to any past communication issues. If they are displeased, you will know very quickly.

In addition, your board president can serve as a communication gauge. A simple meeting to discuss the president's perceptions of the district and perceived district needs will invariably lead into a discussion of superintendent/board relations. In fact, you will probably never have to ask the question directly. If during this meeting you sense that the board was quite satisfied with past practices, ask the board president directly about communication expectations.

As a new superintendent, you must "gauge" communication needs. This is what Fielder (1967) described as situational leadership. Superintendents who are most effective at reading situations and using this information prior to acting increase their success. Do not assume that the board wants something different from the past. Take some time to understand as much as you can about superintendent/board communication before acting. Once you have a good sense of board expectations, you are better prepared to assert your personal style.

Strategy 2: Consider a Board Retreat

Some superintendents have found that a board/administration retreat can be an effective way to kick-start solid working relationships with their school boards. These are typically offered as a service through state school board or superintendent associations or even consultants. However, before choosing to recommend such a process to your board, ensure that you have a good reason for doing so. You will want to make sure that you understand the process thoroughly before suggesting it. You should also "reference check" those who will lead it. If you are not careful, you might actually hurt rather than help communication. Other superintendents can be an excellent reference source.

Strategy 3: Remember That Less May Actually Be More

Although this appears on the surface to be contradictory, it is not. In truth, you can undermine your success through overcommunication. As a new administrator, you need to resist the temptation to be an overcommunicator. Some beginning superintendents mistakenly believe that they can impress their board members by keeping them constantly informed of every detail of district operations. However, you also must ensure they are never surprised.

At first, lots of communication might appear to be a recipe for communication success. Yet, over time, it can be an invitation for board member micromanagement. When you are too free with information, board members begin to believe that their role is to be involved more as managers rather than policy makers. Once you start down this road, it is difficult to turn back.

Rather than communicating everything, three questions to consider are:

- Is it a topic that is intrinsically important?
- Is it an issue about which they are likely to hear?
- Is it something they need to hear about?

If you use these three questions as your initial filter, you can better judge what and what not to communicate.

At the same time, you should always err on the side of less. For example, you could initiate a simple but informative superintendent memo to accompany board meeting materials. If you do, limit it primarily to positive information about the district, alerts about issues that may surface at the meeting, or brief rationales for key administrative recommendations. Avoid providing overly detailed information.

A summary approach, an executive level of information, is best. For example, you may need to notify the board about student suspensions for insubordinate behavior. Board members do not need to know all the details. In most instances, a brief statement is sufficient. If not, it is much easier to increase the detail in the future than to scale it back once you have set the standard. If you use the less versus more approach initially, board members will generally become accustomed to this level of communication.

Strategy 4: Speak Only Positively about Your Board Members

How do you feel when you hear that superintendents, administrators, or even teachers said something negative about you? Does this affect how you feel about them? The same principle applies to superintendent/board relations. You must remain positive or at least neutral when discussing any board member.

As your mother may have warned you, saying something negative about someone may come back "to bite" you. Also, do not assume that, because you are close with certain colleagues or other district employees, they will keep your comments confidential. Always assume that whatever you say will be passed on.

What can complicate this further is that it is easy to develop a personal relationship with certain board members. You might feel as if you can say anything to them and that it will remain between you. This may be true, but it can also be a recipe for career disaster.

You want to remember that it is always good practice to maintain a professional communication style. This means avoiding becoming overly friendly with any board member. Personal conversations about families and outside interests can increase communication. However, negative comments about other board members will put you over the professional line.

Strategy 5: Plan to Manage Conflicts among Board Members

When disagreements or personality clashes among board members surface, you can find yourself in a difficult situation. Avoid thinking you can personally mediate all situations. You might, though, attempt to focus their interactions on the issues rather than personalities. If you are successful, you will help them learn to work together even if they are not friends outside board meetings.

On the other hand, if this is not successful, more direct action is needed. Here is where the board itself should take responsibility for addressing concerns. If more action is needed, ask the board, preferably the board president, to address the concerns. Remind board members that you report to them as an entire board. As such, you are not in a position to mediate board member disagreements. In almost all instances, board members will respect your position.

If conflicts are severe enough, you could consider employing an independent board consultant. They may be able to ask the right questions and push hidden agendas that either you or the board president cannot.

Again, you should make sure that you suggest a competent and knowledgeable consultant based on recommendations from other superintendents who have had similar experiences.

Strategy 6: Learn to "Bite Your Lip"

Although this is not the normal tendency of strong leaders, those who are successful over many years learn how to grin and bear it. If you observe successful leaders in most professions, they tend to remain amazingly calm in the face of crises, even if attacked personally. You should expect that at some point in your superintendency the public and even teachers and board members will criticize you. This frequently happens during school board meetings.

Remember, as Shakespeare once said, discretion is the better part of valor. Superintendents who react emotionally to criticism may feel vindicated for a short period of time. However, in the end, they undermine their own success. When working with your board, you will enhance your working relationship if you can remain calm under the most trying moments. In fact, it is almost always better to accept public or even board member criticism gracefully rather than react spontaneously. If you feel the need to pursue the discussion, do so a day or two later in a private conversation.

What can assist you in difficult situations is your understanding emotional intelligence research. You should consider reading *Emotional Intelligence 2.0* by Travis Bradberry and Jean Greaves. This book will provide you with a better understanding of yourself and others, which will be of great help to you when you are in pressure-packed situations.

Strategy 7: Do Not Be Afraid to Admit When You Do Not Know Something

Do you remember the Shell Answer Man television commercials? At the time, these became synonymous with the expert who always had all the answers. Leading a school district today is very complex. You cannot know everything.

As a beginning superintendent, one way you can lose your credibility rather quickly is to pretend you know something when you do not. If, for example, you are asked unexpectedly at a board meeting to explain the details of a complicated bond sale or specific district program, it is perfectly acceptable to say you do not know all the details. You can research such questions and get back to board members later. They will respect your honesty. This is preferable to either providing incorrect information or talking around the question, hoping they will be satisfied.

Strategy 8: Seek Out Advice

The superintendency can be lonely. Principals often feel a sense of isolation when they move from the teaching ranks into administration (Kersten 2010). These feelings are only exacerbated in the superintendency. As a result, you must be willing to ask for advice. When dealing with superintendent/board relationships, several resources are available to help you better understand how others have succeeded. Here are three to consider.

- Contact other superintendents to discuss their transition experiences. You might be surprised by the positive response you get. Many superintendents will be thrilled that you asked for their advice. Just do not expect them to seek you out. You must make the first move. They can share with you many valuable ideas.
- Join a superintendent mentoring program. Many AASA state affiliates offer mentoring and coaching options for new and even experienced administrators. In these, you are free to ask any questions. You can also share specific problems, seek advice, and talk through sticky board relationship issues.
- Consult publications such as *The School Administrator* that regularly publish articles on superintendent/school board relationships. These will help you understand that you are not the only superintendent who is confronted with superintendent/board relationship challenges. You will also hear how others resolved theirs successfully.

Strategy 9: Focus on the Details

To help instill confidence with board members, focus on details immediately after assuming your position. If you do not, you might see the confidence in your leadership erode rather quickly.

Over your career, have you ever worked for an administrator who was not detail oriented? These types of leaders tend to be poor planners who do not anticipate everything that needs to be done. For example, they may distribute materials to staff members or even the board that are incomplete or even inaccurate.

As superintendent, you can build confidence in your leadership and enhance your board relationships with attention to detail. Probably the most important materials you prepare are for the school board meeting. You want to ensure that these are thorough and accurate. You never want to have board members point out board packet mistakes during the meeting.

Even the most experienced superintendents are not complacent about board materials. They know that thoroughness and accuracy reflect on their perceived performance. To ensure that a board packet is as mistake free as possible, consider the following.

- Assign one of your support staff the responsibility for board packet oversight.
- Be overly involved in the development and review of your first few sets of board materials. You should let your staff members know that you are doing this initially because you want to be thoroughly prepared for the meeting. Otherwise, this can be interpreted as overcontrolling.
- Expect other administrators or key support staff to review all documents prior to distribution to the board. These extra sets of eyes will help minimize mistakes.

Remember that mistakes equate with uncertainty. You can never give too much attention to these details.

Strategy 10: Look for Opportunities to Educate Your Board

Have you ever thought to yourself that being a school bond consultant or even a doctor is not that complicated? Without a lot of experience, you could easily believe that once bond consultants understand the steps in the sale process, it is easy to repeat them again and again. Is this not the same for surgeons? How hard can it be to remove someone's appendix after you have done it a few times?

The problem with this logic is, of course, that most people have very little understanding of what each of these careers requires. From the perspective of an outsider, a bond sale or operation may appear routine on the surface, but in reality they are actually very complex.

Superintendents, too, face similar challenges to doctors and bond consultants. Those unfamiliar with what superintendents actually do often wonder if they even need to work during the summer. What can superintendents possibly do during the summer without children and teachers in attendance?

Some board members, especially those relatively new to the board, may have a similar impression. Because they are removed from the day-to-day operations of the district, they may believe that district administration is a simple management task. Teachers, they think, do all the real work. Superintendents just manage them.

As a beginning superintendent or even an experienced one, you can enhance your relationship with your board of education by educating them. Rather than ensuring that district leadership always appears quite simple, look for opportunities to help them appreciate the complexity inherent in your position.

One way successful superintendents accomplish this is by conducting educational sessions for board members. These are typically offered in two formats.

New Board Member Orientation

One of the most effective ways to educate your board is through a formal board orientation process. As a new superintendent, the timing of the board election may not align directly with your appointment. However, it is very possible that you might replace a board member during your first year. A board orientation process allows you to proactively reach out to underinformed board members. It also allows you to demonstrate the complexity of district management and showcase yourself and other administrators as true experts.

A proven process includes at least three sessions on topics such as the following:

- History of the school district
- District philosophy
- Role of the board of education
- Board meeting structure
- District/unit goals and goal setting process
- Curriculum and instructional programs
- District finances
- Insurance programs
- Building and grounds
- Personnel administration, including compensation programs
- Collective bargaining

You should involve at least your board president and one other board member, especially for the discussion of topics related to the board of education's functioning or policy role. They can take the lead on the discussion, which is preferable since this demonstrates the connection between the board and administration. Also, by inviting other board members to attend, you will also educate them further. Be careful to check your state Open Meeting Act requirements to avoid any political entanglements.

You can demonstrate your personal leadership by presenting some portion of the workshops yourself. However, this process also allows you to showcase your other administrators. For example, by having your school business official present the financial data, you empower the administrator with your board. Since school business managers are very knowledgeable on all areas of school finance, they are well equipped to demonstrate the complexity of the topic. By doing this, you also show how competent your administrative staff is, which is a compliment to your leadership!

An important element of the board orientation process is the material preparation. You and your other administrators should develop in-depth materials for distribution before each session. You will find that board members who thought district leadership was unsophisticated quickly see just how complex it is.

As you conduct the orientation, you also want to make the point with your board members that you do not expect them to master everything presented. Rather, ask them to treat these sessions as an introduction to district operations. You should tell them that they will understand each topic more fully as their term unfolds. Also, you should point out that the depth of information in the handouts was intentional. They now have detailed materials to which they can refer during the year.

Focused Workshops

In addition to board orientations, another way to educate your board is to build information sessions into board meetings or as special activities. It is important to remember that even board members who have served for some time may have forgotten key information. Because they only see most topics sporadically, they cannot be expected to remember much detail. By identifying key topics and discussing them with your board, you not only help them understand them better, but you also reinforce any message you want to convey.

Strategy 11: Collaborate with Your Board President on the Board Meeting Agenda

In most school districts, school board members view the school board president as the liaison to the district administration. As a beginning superintendent, you want to acknowledge and support this role. One way to accomplish this is to plan the school board meeting agenda together.

Here are guidelines to consider.

- Meet with your president and possibly vice president to plan the agenda. A breakfast session would be ideal since you can accomplish the task in an informal setting.
- Establish an expectation that any board member with a possible agenda item needs to contact you or the board president before the agenda setting meeting.

In addition to planning the agenda, you should touch base with your board president at least the evening before the meeting to ensure you are on the same page. This will reinforce the president's role while helping you establish a good working relationship.

SUMMARY

This chapter has examined both important principles and practices associated with effective superintendent/school board relationships. Discussed first were myths associated with superintendent job security, a common concern for those seeking the superintendency. Also presented were a series of strategies that both beginning and experienced superintendents can use to develop positive working relationships with their boards of education.

SIX

Establishing Relationships Within the School District

One of the immediate adjustments you will have to make as you transition into the superintendency is establishing positive relationships with various district employee groups. As principal, your contacts tended to be focused on the school's teachers, support staff, students, and parents. Even if you served as an assistant superintendent, you probably had fairly regular contact with teachers and support staff.

As superintendent, you will discover that your scope of contacts is much broader but more superficial. Even in smaller school districts, relationships with school-based employees will be less personal. As a result, do not be surprised if others respond to you differently just because you are the superintendent.

In some ways, you may actually see this as a plus, primarily because you are not the direct supervisor for most school employees. As a result, your relationships with them will tend to be more positive in focus. In addition, in your role you will interact more casually with teachers and staff. This is in contrast to other administrators who are more frequently responsible for delivering any bad news.

In school districts, principals are the primary frontline supervisors. They are responsible for most day-to-day personnel and student issues. However, because you may be accustomed to daily supervision, one challenge you may face as superintendent is letting go of your tendency to be everyone's direct supervisor. However, if you do, you will learn that often it is far more effective to delegate than intervene.

Unfortunately, sometimes new superintendents try to act as if they are district-wide principals. This tendency is actually quite natural. For much of their careers, they were take-charge, school-level leaders who were problem solvers. They were expected to jump into any number of school situations. They felt a sense of satisfaction resolving them.

As superintendent, though, this type of action will undermine your success as well as that of your administrators. You need to fight the urge to step in to solve school and district issues for which others are responsible. If you do not, before long, others will bypass their direct supervisors to seek help directly from you. As a new superintendent, this may actually feel good at first because you will believe that you are making a tangible difference. Yet, over a relatively short period of time, you will create district inefficiencies. You will also alienate your administrators.

As you may have done when you were a principal, begin by directing problems to those at the level where they should be resolved. For example, if you are approached by a parent regarding a classroom grading policy, you should direct the parent back to the principal or teacher. If you do not, before long the word will circulate that, if anyone has a problem, they should go directly to the superintendent. You can let the parent know that, if their issue cannot be resolved, you will be happy to meet with them.

At the same time, some successful superintendents let parents know that they delegate most school-related decisions to their building administrators. As superintendents, they only review decisions that are clearly wrong. This approach can be effective in ensuring that school issues are resolved primarily at the school level.

WORKING WITH DISTRICT ADMINISTRATORS

As superintendent, you must accept the reality that you are no longer just one of the administrators. You are now viewed as the "head boss." As a result, your relationships with other administrators will be different.

Yes, you will still be a member of the administrative team. However, other administrators will view you differently. This is normal and natural. Every organization has a leadership hierarchy. Other administrators will see you as their evaluator. This is similar to how teachers viewed you when you were their principal, especially if you have a substantial impact on their salary increases. They know that you will make decisions about their future employment. As a result, they will respond to you differently than they do with other administrative colleagues.

Once you accept this difference, you are ready to focus more effectively on building positive relationships with your administrators. As superintendent, you can create an effective administrative team that respects you as its leader. Below are several important strategies you may want to consider as you begin working with your administrators.

Strategy 1: Expect Collaboration Rather Than Competition

Successful school district administrative teams are collaborative. Competition among administrators is generally unproductive and discourages cooperation. In fact, it can impede progress toward meeting district goals. As the new superintendent, you should immediately establish an expectation for collaboration. You should state in no uncertain terms that you expect them to work together as an administrative team. You should especially make a point of telling any new administrators that collaboration with colleagues is essential. If you do not, they will try to second guess what you want. Clarity of expectations is critical.

Establishing a collaborative administrative team may be a challenge in certain school districts. You may find yourself employed in a school district where competition among administrators is encouraged. In fact, administrators may have been hired because they valued competition.

If so, it will take longer for you to create a cooperative team atmosphere. You will need to be persistent. Although this may sound counterintuitive, in some instances you may need to assert yourself as the district leader. This means telling them individually your direct expectations. In some extreme cases, you may even have to terminate an administrator who refuses to comply.

At the same time, requesting and living administrative collaboration, as a superintendent, are quite distinct. You have probably known administrators who talked a good game but acted differently. Remember that you, too, must be collaborative if you expect others to follow your lead.

One way to demonstrate collaborative leadership is to create opportunities for your administrators to be actively involved in decision-making. For example, you might establish an administrative meeting culture in which everyone is encouraged to express their opinions freely. If you do, you should clarify upfront whether a final decision is yours or theirs. As part of this process, you should encourage them to disagree with you respectfully. This will discourage them from expressing opinions just to please you. If you do, though, you will need to accept their opinions without becoming defensive. In the end, this type of collaboration can help you avoid hasty or poor decisions while contributing to administrative cohesiveness.

You might use a consensus administrative decision-making model. Superintendents who use this approach foster brainstorming and encourage variant opinions as long as they are made in the spirit of cooperation. They also make decisions by consensus. That is, they discuss something until all can either agree or least everyone is comfortable enough to not block the decision. Such a process requires time and patience to implement. However, if done well, it can lead to a more collegial and focused administrative team spirit.

Strategy 2: Treat All Administrators Equally

Undoubtedly, you will find yourself gravitating toward some administrators over others. This is natural. However, if you want to maximize your administrative relationships, you must treat all equitably. This means never leaving the impression that you favor one over another.

Have you ever seen principals who received special treatment from their superintendents? Superintendents who do so can damage their relationships with their administrative team. Sometimes this can be as simple as focusing their group conversation toward only one individual. Other times it emerges in the form of public praising. If you want to recognize someone personally, do so in person. If you do it visibly, you can create jealousies among administrators. It is always best to avoid leaving the impression that one administrator is ever favored over another.

Strategy 3: Try to Get to Know Each Administrator on a More Personal Level

Although your relationships with your administrators will always have a supervisor-supervisee component, they can nonetheless be personal. Some superintendents only establish artificial personal relationships with their administrative team members. They never let their administrators really get to know them. Such superintendents often employ this as a defense mechanism. They worry that, someday, they may have to discipline or even fire them. As a result, they never allow anyone to get too close to them. In the long-run, this approach, unfortunately, may limit spontaneous interactions and reduce openness of communication between the superintendent and administrative staff.

As a new superintendent, you can begin cultivating positive, productive relationships with your administrative team members by:

- Finding regular opportunities to meet with them individually. This can be as simple as dropping into their offices for informal chats without any specific agenda. This will help you avoid creating the impression that the only time you visit is when you have a business-related agenda;
- Showing a genuine interest in them as individuals. Encourage them to discuss their families and social activities. Allow enough time to really visit so you do not send the message that your interest is superficial;
- Sharing information about yourself and your family without becoming too familiar. This will help you break through the business-only barrier;
- Reaching out to support them with any problems or special needs. This may mean being flexible with certain work expectations or meeting requirements;

- Being a good listener. Superintendents who are less successful relationship builders tend to be overtalkers. They dominate conversations. By listening more and talking less, you can cultivate much more genuine relationships;
- Encouraging other administrators to organize social events that are inclusive of all administrators. Highly successful superintendents discourage noninclusive behavior. For example, if administrators organize dinner get-togethers before board meetings, they should not exclude some members. You want to do whatever you can to discourage partisan behaviors; and
- Hosting social gatherings yourself for administrators and spouses/ friends. Look for opportunities to bring your administrators together. Getting to know each of their families better often leads to more comfortable and productive work relationships among administrators. By the way, if you can provide all the food and drink, so much the better.

Strategy 4: Maintain a Half-Full Perspective

A positive attitude can be infectious. Think about the type of people you would rather be around. Are they complainers? They probably are not. Most people enjoy working with leaders who tend to be upbeat. If you become too focused on problems, it will affect administrative morale. If at all possible, try to be upbeat and calm even in the face of conflict and negativity.

Strategy 5: Avoid Know-It-All Behavior

Leaders who must be constant centers of attention rarely develop functional administrative teams. Know-it-all superintendents spend too much time telling others how much they know and how best to accomplish everything. These superintendents also tend to be closed to others' ideas. This is a tried and tested way to quickly turn off others. You would be well served to be the type of leader who operates as a team member, not the one who must tell others what to do.

Strategy 6: Look for Opportunities to Compliment Each of Your Administrators to Key Staff Members, Parents, and Board Members

When someone makes a compliment about a person, the person complimented often hears about it. When you have conversations with your board members, parents, and staff members, look for opportunities to interject positive comments about your administrators. Because these are more natural and conversation-based, they will not create the competition among administrators that public praising does. This is a good strategy to enhance the credibility of your administrators while letting them know you appreciate their work. At some point, you can be assured that they will hear you said something encouraging about them.

Strategy 7: Build in a Regular Process to Review Your Administrators' Goals

As is true of almost any successful leader, if you emphasize something, it tends to be accomplished. This same principle is important in helping your administrators meet their goals. If at all possible, try to meet with each of your administrators once a month in their offices to review their goals and evidence of progress. If your district is large, you may want to share this responsibility with other district-level administrators. Just by meeting with them and having a focused conversation, you show your commitment to improvement and raise the achievement bar.

WORKING WITH TEACHERS

Teachers truly are influential district employees. Parents and board members typically see them as district barometers. Because they work directly with children, others listen closely to what they have to say, including their impressions of the district and the superintendent. As a result, as the new superintendent, you want to focus on establishing comfortable working relationships with teachers. If you do, you can enhance your early success. Here are several strategies you should consider to help ensure positive relationships with the teaching staff.

Strategy 1: Make a Positive First Impression

Establishing productive relationships actually begins the moment you meet teachers during the interview process. Although these first impressions will be modified continually during your tenure in the school district, a good initial impression will smooth your transition into the superintendency.

As the new district leader, you are basically an unknown. Yes, some will have heard something about you before you start. However, most will form their own opinions based on what you say and do, especially during your first year. Look for ways to show that you are someone that they can count on for strong leadership.

Strategy 2: Speak Positively about the Teaching Profession

It is easy for superintendents to fall into negative teacher talk when teachers and teachers' unions make demands on them. As a new superintendent, you must resist the temptation to let such issues skew your perspective of the profession. If you do not, it will hurt your relationships with teachers.

As a beginning superintendent, you can build your reputation with faculty members by asserting yourself as a professional spokesperson. This means being a champion of education and teachers. You want to make sure that you are seen as the type of leader who values teaching and recognizes it as a noble profession. In essence, become a spokesman for the importance of teaching and teachers.

Strategy 3: Avoid Central Office Isolation

Too often superintendents get caught up in district-level problems and daily responsibilities. These are, of course, important. However, you cannot allow them to be all-consuming. Rather, you should make one of your priorities finding ways to interact with teachers on a personal level. Here are some suggestions.

- Make a commitment to visit each school on a regular basis. Vary the time of day to increase your exposure to as many teachers as possible.
- Drop into classrooms briefly during school visits. Also, do not forget to spend some time socializing in the faculty lounge.
- Find time, if at all possible, to send a note to teachers you visited. Keep the note short and specific, and focused on something positive you observed. Most teachers value this level of personal recognition.
- Plan school visits during lunch time. Remember to order a school lunch! Use this time to socialize with faculty members so they get to know you as an individual.
- Meet with principals to learn about each faculty member. Focus on their teaching responsibilities and other interesting personal information. Avoid asking principals to assess teaching performance. What you learn will help you interact more naturally with faculty members.
- Sit in periodically on various committee meetings. However, make it clear that you are there as an observer, not a participant. These visits will provide you with a broader perspective of the district. If asked later by board members or parents about district activities, you will be able to discuss them confidently. This also sends the message to teachers that you are interested in what they and their students are doing.
- Make a point of attending every possible social event you can. In large school districts, this may be difficult. If you do, though, you will succeed in showing others that you are a visible, approachable administrator.
- Look for opportunities to bring all district staff together for social events. In tight financial times, this may be a challenge. Nonethe-

less, when teachers see you in these informal settings, they cannot help but feel more connected to you.

Strategy 4: Be an Informed Leader

Since teachers will form impressions of you based on minimal contact, you want to make the most of the time that you have with them. Consider for a moment the impression you want to make. Is it sufficient to be merely friendly and visible? Or do you want them to see you as an educational leader?

Superintendents can be liked by faculty members but not particularly respected. Have you ever worked with an administrator who was well liked but perceived as a weak school or district leader? To truly be a well-respected superintendent, others must see you as educationally up-to-date. Conversations with teachers must at times go beyond personal topics. You must also be confident and knowledgeable enough to express informed opinions and discuss educational issues.

Strategy 5: Value Teacher Ideas

To succeed as a school administrator today, you must be open to others' ideas. The days of the authoritarian superintendent are gone. Teachers, in particular, expect to be consulted on issues related to their responsibilities. This raises the question: How do you involve teachers while maintaining your decision-making authority?

The first step is to define which decisions are primarily yours and which should be highly influenced by teachers. For example, you would not consult teachers on whether or not to conduct fire drills. But you would want them to weigh in on how best to implement the Common Core Standards.

Teachers in the district probably already have both formal and informal opportunities to collaborate with administrators. In addition, though, you may want to consider one or more of the following approaches.

Superintendent Advisory Councils

One way to let teachers know that you value their ideas is to create a superintendent advisory council. These usually consist of a representative group of district stakeholders, including administrators, parents, and teachers. Since these advisory groups are administrative committees, they should not include board members. Otherwise, they become too closely linked to board committees and also encourage micromanagement.

As a new superintendent, you want to think through the advisory council process thoroughly before deciding to start one. Since you will be initiating it, you have the opportunity to structure both the committee membership and the logistics. Remember that once you set the focus and parameters, you will find it more difficult to change them.

Before you decide to create a superintendent advisory council, answer these questions:

- What will be the purpose of the council?
- Will it meet as needed or be a standing committee?
- What will be the committee membership?
- How will members be selected?
- How long will they serve?
- How often will the group meet?
- What will be the committee ground rules?
- What does "advise" mean?
- What are the expected outcomes?
- How will the agenda be determined?
- How and to whom will the information from the council be disseminated?

Advisory councils are most effective when the process is well thought through before implementation. It is also advisable to start small. That is, plan to have fewer rather than more council members and meet less frequently. Remember that it is always easier to expand the advisory council than reduce it.

Faculty Involvement

One mistake new superintendents can make is soliciting input only from teachers who they enjoy being around and/or who will agree with them. Unfortunately, this is a sure way to earn a reputation as a controlling superintendent. What is less comfortable but preferable is inviting broad-based input from individuals who may disagree with you or even be publicly critical.

As you begin your new position, it is advisable to include some individuals on committees or into advisory processes who are perceived by others as less supportive. Although this may make interactions less comfortable at times, you cannot be accused of stacking the deck with only supporters. As superintendent, you must adjust to the reality that inherent in your position is some level of conflict. However, if you can calmly accept diverse opinions before making decisions, you will enhance your leadership reputation.

In-School Advisory Sessions

Another way to show teachers that you value their ideas is to make yourself available for in-school advisory sessions. These can be as simple as letting teachers know that you will be in a particular location in the school on a certain day for conversation about anything on their minds. When you visit, you want to schedule yourself sufficient time to allow anyone interested to meet.

Another approach is to structure advisory sessions around a particular topic. For example, if the school district is considering a change in the grading policy or a new school day structure, you could use in-session advisory sessions to gather faculty perspectives. What is most important about this process is that you are reaching out to them.

Share the Stage

Another strategy to show you value teachers' ideas is to acknowledge their involvement. If you integrate one of their ideas into an initiative, make sure that you acknowledge it as theirs. If you are discussing district directions, look for opportunities to point out teachers' contributions. By sharing the stage, you can broaden your support base among teachers while sending the message that they were heard.

WORKING WITH SUPPORT STAFF

In addition to administrators and teachers, another important employee group is the district support staff. Many live in the community. Similar to teachers, they can make or break a new superintendent's reputation with their comments. Since they serve in any variety of support roles, others see them as even less connected to the administration than they see teachers. But when they share stories about what is going on in classrooms and cafeterias, as well as on buses, their friends listen. Others in the community will be especially open to their impressions of the new superintendent.

Some of the most influential support personnel are the district office staff. The most important person may be the superintendent's administrative assistant. What they share informally with others inside and outside the district about their comfort level with you, your work ethic, and management skills can affect your reputation quickly. If these key staff members say positive things about you, they can enhance your success.

Winning staff support is not difficult if you make it one of your priorities. Here are several strategies to consider.

Strategy 1: Treat Them with Respect

One sure way to alienate your support staff is to focus too much on administrators and teachers while taking them for granted. Have you ever heard custodians or secretaries say that a certain administrator treat-ed them as if they were second-class citizens? If so, you observed how their attitudes about the administration are negatively affected.

If you want to win their support, treat them with the same level of respect that you do your certificated staff. Administrators who earn reputations as poor relationship builders largely do so by ignoring support staff members. Too often support staff members believe that teachers and administrators perceive them as less important. To counter this perception, think of them as just as valuable to the school district as other employees. If you treat them like you would want someone to treat you, you will be successful.

Strategy 2: Keep Them in the Loop

Superintendents spend a great deal of time and energy ensuring that boards of education and certificated staff members are very involved in establishing and implementing district priorities. In contrast, some superintendents do not involve support staff at all. As the new superintendent, a helpful relationship-building strategy is to ensure that support staff members are provided with a good understanding of district priorities as well as their role in achieving them. This includes district-wide emails and other communications. Even though they may not actually be involved in setting district priorities, they should be included in the communication process. This will make them feel more connected to the district and also to you.

Strategy 3: Get to Know Them on a Personal Level

You can never emphasize personal connections enough. Just as you would with your administrators and certificated staff, make a point of getting to know support staff members on a personal level. This includes seeking them out much as you do teachers and administrators when you visit district facilities. This may mean even more to these employees because, in some districts, they are not engaged. Simply stopping in their work area regularly or getting to know something personal about them or their families will mean a great deal. This is especially good strategy for you as a new superintendent because most support staff will not expect you to do this.

Strategy 4: Look for Ways to Recognize their Contributions

As with anyone, support staff members appreciate recognition. Again, you want to avoid individual public praise that can create unhealthy jealousies. However, well-placed, individual recognition can have a positive effect on someone's perception of you.

At the same time, successful superintendents look for ways to build broad-based, public recognition activities into district traditions. Some time-tested activities at which you take an active role may be:

- Providing service awards programs, which may include bonuses linked to years of service.
- Displaying service recognition plaques in school and/or district offices.
- Scheduling special events such as a thank-you breakfast for custodians just before the start of the school year.
- Organizing end-of-year retirement teas that include both certificated and support staff recognition.
- Acknowledging general support staff contributions at institute days and other district events.

In essence, look for creative ways to let support staff members know that you appreciate them. In the long run, this can pay significant relationship dividends.

WORKING WITH UNIONS

One of the real challenges you will face is working with unions. You need to recognize that establishing a productive relationship with them is to your advantage in the long run. You may have to fight the tendency to avoid or resist union leadership. One way to establish a positive working relationship is to commit to monthly meetings. In fact, take the lead and suggest this approach. If you are fair-minded and open to issues, generally you will be able to develop a good working relationship. In fact, you will be much more likely to resolve problems before grievances are filed.

SUMMARY

One of the most important elements of a new superintendent's success is establishing positive relationships with district employees. Those who do dramatically enhance their effectiveness early in their superintendencies. This chapter has discussed the importance of relationship building with the four critical groups: administrators, teachers, support staff, and unions. A variety of strategies as well as practical suggestions were presented.

SEVEN

Building Relationships Outside the School District

For new superintendents, building positive relationships with those outside the school district is nearly as important as building those within the district. Unlike other administrators who are primarily internally focused, superintendents must work effectively with many individuals and groups that may have minimal, if any, direct day-to-day connections to the schools. As you begin your superintendency, you must recognize the important role these individuals will play in your success.

As superintendent, you will often have little regular interaction with those not directly involved with your schools. In fact, superintendents usually view this as an indicator that there are few burning district issues. However, when residents do come forward, they are not usually there to compliment you. Rather, they tend to appear when they want something or have a concern. As the district leader, how well you prepare and respond to potential issues can impact your personal success.

As you step into the superintendency, you should recognize that relationship building with those outside the district actually begins before you meet many constituents. In fact, you can minimize future conflicts and therefore enhance relationships if you are proactive and reach out to them.

Here are several strategies you might want to consider both to minimize potential problems as well as build positive, productive relationships.

Strategy 1: Evaluate the Efficacy of Existing District Policies and
Accompanying Administrative Procedures

As you begin your superintendency, you would be wise to build some time into your schedule to review existing school board policies and administrative procedures. Do not wait until an issue develops. However, this does not necessarily mean initiating an extensive school board review process. If not needed, a too formalized review process can lead to excessive board involvement or even micromanagement. As a new superintendent, start with an administrative review.

To begin, rely on your own experiences. Identify issues that emerged in your former districts. It is probable that you will experience similar ones in your new position. Also, seek advice from more experienced superintendents. They have years of personal experience and have watched other colleagues grapple with any number of policy-related problems. They can pinpoint areas to which you should pay special attention.

Some of the most common policy issues that superintendents face include requests to use district facilities or permission to distribute materials. Others are requests for school district support for community groups or special programs. To illustrate this, consider this question. How would you respond to a local resident's request to rent space in one of your district's schools for a weekly worship service? These types of issues can emerge spontaneously. With well-considered policies and procedures, you can minimize potential conflicts and build good relationships.

In some districts, policies and accompanying procedures may not have been examined for years. Therefore, during your review, look for potential problem areas or discrepancies with current or good practice. You should also include your administrative team members in this process. They understand the district's history and can offer various perspectives.

If you determine that a more extensive process is necessary, you might consider allocating funds for a review by a school district attorney. You could also use services provided by professional associations such as your state AASA affiliate or school board organization. Remember that policy and procedure adjustments are much easier to make when you are proactive rather than reactive.

Strategy 2: Reach Out to Your Community

When school districts need more resources or are faced with a crisis, it is often too late to expect automatic community support if you have not established strong relationships. As you begin your superintendency, consider ways to bring the general public into your schools. This will allow them to see firsthand what their tax dollars are supporting. It is also a way for them to get to know you.

One way to accomplish this is to offer community tours of school district facilities when classes are in session. Too often residents or even some parents, who are not in their local schools regularly, assume that problems they have heard about in the state and national news plague your schools. They may believe that drug and discipline problems permeate even your elementary schools. The best way to discount these perceptions is to bring community members and parents into your schools while classes are in session. No matter how much you promote your schools at meetings or through web or print materials, nothing is more powerful than direct experience.

As superintendent, you can show your leadership by establishing a community visitation program. Here are steps to consider.

- Make sure that you discuss the idea with your school board before moving forward. You want them to understand its purposes and focus. You should also consider involving board members in tours. School board members will tend to respond very positively to any activity that shows you are reaching out to the community.
- Ensure that teachers and support staff are onboard with the program.
- Select two or three dates in cooperation with your administrative team to host community visits.
- Advertise the program through parent organizations. In this way, you also become more connected with parent groups.
- Flood the local community with news about the program. Use available district communications vehicles as well as local media. A bonus is that such an event allows you to establish a relationship with your local newspaper reporter around a positive rather than negative issue.
- Establish a schedule for the day that begins with an overview of your district. Make sure you include introductions of administrative team members who will guide tours. During this session, which may be conducted in your district office, discuss school district goals and priorities. This is your way of saying that you are there to provide the best education possible for district children. By the way, make sure that you meet and greet everyone personally. Do not forget to provide refreshments!
- Arrange for a school bus to transport participants from the district office to each school site. If possible, ride with them. In large school districts, you may have to schedule separate buses to individual schools.

- Have each principal serve as the school's tour guide. Of course, you want to meet with your administrators beforehand to plan each tour thoroughly to ensure a seamless, focused message.
- Following the tours, invite all visitors and administrators to a luncheon or reception at the district office. This is a good opportunity for socializing. It will allow you to answer any lingering questions. The event will be especially appreciated by your senior citizen participants who may view the schools mainly as the source of their property tax increases.

In almost all instances, these visits will be a great public relations tool. Participants will see firsthand the quality of education you provide. You will also put to rest any fears and misconceptions they may have had. When they see teachers teaching and students working, they will disassociate your schools from those highlighted in the media. Better yet, you will have created a new set of school district ambassadors who will freely discuss their experiences with others. Think about how powerful this can be, especially if influential community members leave having had a positive experience.

Strategy 3: Look for Opportunities to Establish School District–Business Partnerships

Too often local business leaders believe that the only reason superintendents seek them out for partnerships is because they want a donation. An effective way to bridge this gap and build mutually supportive relationships is to think common needs. That is, look for opportunities to link local businesses with your educational programs. Here are some examples you might want to consider.

Bank at School Program

Local bankers are often eager to increase their visibility in the community. At the same time, school districts typically introduce students to very basic personal financing topics during the elementary grades. One way to meld these together is to begin a bank at school program in cooperation with the help of a local bank. However, before beginning a program, make sure you understand your community. This concept may not be viable if you have too many banks who want to participate.

However, if feasible, you can begin with a partnership agreement with a local bank and one or more schools. Under this format, bankers assist students in setting up savings accounts. They also visit schools on a regular schedule to accept deposits. Teachers contribute by providing students with saving guidance. Through such a win-win partnership program, students are introduced to the importance of regular savings.

Poetry Night

A good way to extend student poetry writing is to work with a local bookstore to initiate a school poetry night partnership program. Working with the bookstore manager, you can designate special evenings during which students read their poetry at the store. Customers, parents, other students, board members, and other community members are invited to the "open mic" night. Bookstores not only increase their presence in the community but help you highlight the importance of poetry in your language curriculum.

Fall/Spring Fest

What better way is there to bring your entire school community together with the support of local businesses than to host a fall or spring fest? Consider scheduling the fest after school at one of your district facilities. If weather permits, an outside venue will enhance the community feel of the experience. Examples of activities you might want to offer include:

- Welcoming comments from you and your board president as well as parent organization representatives or even the mayor.
- Opportunities for local food vendors to set up booths to sell food and refreshments.
- Booths sponsored by parent organizations that offer fest guests opportunities to participate in free craft and game activities.
- Free game booths with small prizes paid for by the school board. You can contract with a commercial midway game company for this service.
- Free cotton candy spun by the district administrators and board members.

The scope and focus of this event is only limited by your creativity and available district funds.

Chamber of Commerce Partnerships

Business leaders know that good schools equate with increased business activity. As a result, local Chambers of Commerce are often eager to develop school-business partnerships. These help them build community support while increasing their visibility. Some even have education committees focused on relationships with local schools.

Although these partnerships can take many forms, one to consider is asking the chamber to create an annual outstanding teacher and student award program. This is a good way for the business community to increase its involvement in your schools in such a way that they simultaneously endorse one of your education priorities.

Strategy 4: Develop Good Working Relationships with Other Local Government Units

School districts do not operate in isolation, but rather must work periodically with other governmental units. As such, it is important to recognize that both have an interest in the other's success. For example, when a student brings a gun to school, you count on the police department to assist you with the actual response to the problem. Later, you will both need to depend on each other for support as you manage the aftermath. If you have a gas leak emergency, fire department response is essential. Similarly, the fire department may need your assistance in developing an emergency community response plan. Finally, you could be asked to work collaboratively with village officials to coordinate infrastructure improvements as part of a school construction project.

Because of the importance of establishing a collaborative, professional relationship with other local governmental units, you should reach out to them early in your tenure. You want to invite each agency's chief administrator to meet with you. Meet them on their "turf." Keep the session short, possibly only fifteen minutes. As the new superintendent, ask them what you need to do to be successful in the community.

Also, during your time together make a point of letting them know how much you are looking forward to working with them. You should also ask them to explain how they have worked with the school district in the past. Encourage them to offer suggestions on how both organizations can work together for even more efficiencies.

As is true with almost all relationships, the more accommodating you are and the more other governmental unit administrators get to know and trust you, the better the relationship. You should avoid the ego trap. You will hurt your relationships with these administrators if you are too egocentric. You want to make every effort to be perceived as a colleague and not a competitor.

Remember that city governmental agencies, too, have boards to which they report. Each has individual priorities, some of which may not always align well with your school district needs. For example, the downtown business district may have fallen on tough economic times. The village board and local businessmen may be seeking a tax increment financing district (TIF). At the same time, you might be worried that a TIF will mean lost tax dollars. Rather than immediately attacking them for even considering a TIF, it is far more effective to try to understand their perspective. However, do not be afraid to negotiate TIF terms. If you are open-minded and cooperative, you might even find them amenable to modifying the TIF agreement to provide some economic relief for the school district.

In addition, some collaborative relationships provide economic benefits for both parties. It is quite common to reach an agreement with the park district that includes free use of district facilities in exchange for landscaping services. As the new superintendent, you may want to begin the conversation.

Strategy 5: Reach Out to the PTA/PTO

The most influential groups you will deal with are the local school parent organizations. They are highly vested in the children's education and, as a result, will be inclined to support your educational initiatives. However, you need to find ways to let them get to know you and your priorities.

A successful way to do this is to ask each of your principals to invite you to at least one parent board meeting a year. When you attend, ask parents to provide you with their priorities and any concerns or other thoughts they have about the schools. Your role is to be a good listener, although you will be able to share specific information about the district as part of the conversation.

Strategy 6: Connect with Key Community Groups

In additional to general community and governmental leaders, you should consider inviting other influential community leaders into your school district. The more each feels connected with the district and you, the greater the likelihood of increasing your community support base. The best time to do so is during your first year. At that point, they are most curious about the school district leadership change. You also will be perceived as reaching out to them because of a mutual interest rather than because you have a specific request.

One mistake beginning superintendents can make is only contacting influential community leaders when they want something. For example, if you wait until you need to pass an operating rate referendum, you may be perceived as an opportunist. A better approach is to have regular communication with these key individuals including such often forgotten groups as clergy, historical society leaders, and real estate agents.

These individuals have a vested interest in your school district's success. They can also provide an independent level of support when others challenge your curriculum or raise questions about district and school leadership. If they support your district tax increase proposal, you increase your chances for success. It is to your advantage to develop a good working relationship with them. If they know and trust you, they can be some of your greatest supporters.

Earning their support can be as simple as hosting a meeting a year. Similar to other community visitation programs, use your schools as your showpiece. Whether they lead religious groups, volunteer for community organizations, or sell homes, they value good schools.

Consider developing an agenda in which you showcase your district's priorities and successes. Build in time for each person to meet your district administrators and perhaps one or two board members. Remember to ask them for their impressions of your district schools so the session is more a conversation than a sales pitch. Finally, ensure that a tour of at least one of your schools is part of the agenda.

Strategy 7: Get to Know County/State Education Officials

Some superintendents only contact county and state agency administrators when they have a problem or need help. If you spend some time getting acquainted with each organization and its key administrators, you will find them more responsive when you need to call. Even more important, when you are in a bind, they may bend over backwards to assist you.

Avoid the temptation to be a county or state critic. Little is gained but quite a bit can be lost if you are perceived as negative. It is important to remember that these leaders can do a lot to help or hinder your leadership. Even if, for example, an administrator at your state education agency is dictatorial or rigid, you will be more successful working with them if you try hard to build a good relationship.

Strategy 8: Recognize the Importance of Building Relationships with Leaders of Professional Administrative Organizations

As a beginning superintendent, you will be extremely busy. You cannot be active in every local, state, and national superintendent organization. At the least, though, participate in your local, township, or county superintendent association. Beyond that, it is important to choose those in which you will be most active. As you get involved, remember that how you are perceived by other superintendents and organization leaders will affect your reputation. Here are some suggestions on how to be perceived as a contributing member.

- Try to attend all local, township, or county superintendent association meetings. However, avoid volunteering to take a leadership role initially. Rather, focus on being an active discussant.
- Be on time to all meetings. Arriving late sends the message that you are either disorganized or that you think your time is more valuable than others'.

- Avoid any hint of favoritism. Try to get to know all superintendents. You want to develop a reputation as someone everyone likes and respects.
- Be a worker. Volunteer to participate in initiatives as time permits. Offer to help whenever possible.
- Be a leadership supporter rather than a critic. Consider for a moment how you feel when someone criticizes you.
- Do not be afraid to voice your opinions but do so in a nonconfrontational way.
- Show willingness to compromise.
- Volunteer to organize social events that bring superintendents together.

Having positive collegial relationships with other superintendents and professional organization leaders may prove to be important to your success when you least expect it.

Strategy 9: Cultivate Communication with State Elected Officials

As you know, public education is the responsibility of the state. As such, elected officials wield final decision-making authority on any number of education requirements. Most do not come from an education background and, similar to most parents, rely on their own experiences with their children's education. They also listen closely to their constituents.

As superintendent, you should make a point of getting to know your state representatives and their key staff members. Then, if you have a concern or a question, you can contact them directly. Also, if they know and respect you, you may be the person they call for help understanding and interpreting potential legislation that impacts their legislative districts.

Strategy 10: Prepare Yourself for Negative Responses

As much as you try to reach out to others, you cannot control their responses. As superintendent, you will discover that you have to accept the reality that some people are closed to relationship building. No matter how friendly and responsive you are, you may not be able to build a positive relationship with them. However, the more you avoid overreacting to them while still attempting to be responsive, the greater the chances that you can minimize negative interactions with them.

SUMMARY

Beginning superintendents should never underestimate the importance of relationship building with those who have minimal day-to-day contact with their school districts. This chapter offered specific strategies new superintendents can use to build relationships with individuals and groups with little, if any, direct contact with their school districts.

The importance of updating school district policies and administrative procedures was discussed. Also explored were ways to build support in the community through school visitation programs and partnership activities. Suggestions were offered on ways to work well with local governmental units, parent organizations, community groups, and state and county education agencies. Finally, the role of the superintendent in professional organizations was discussed. Suggestions were offered on how new superintendents could best establish themselves as respected, productive association members.

EIGHT

Making Principal and Teacher Selection Your Top Priority

As a school administrator, you probably do not have to be convinced how important administrator and teacher selection is to your success. You know that, if you employ competent, personable, and flexible individuals, your job will be much easier. Just as teachers spend far more time working with students who are socially or behaviorally challenged, administrators also spend more time dealing with poor employees.

As a new superintendent, you will inherit a very heterogeneous group of employees. If you are fortunate, you may step into a district that has hired well over a long period of time. But more likely, you will find a broad spectrum of administrators and teachers with whom you will need to learn to work effectively.

Yet, even in the beginning of your tenure or at least during your first year, you will have the opportunity to lead the selection of some teachers and maybe even administrators. You should consider this your opportunity to have an immediate impact on the district.

MINIMIZING HIRING MISTAKES

Unfortunately, beginning and even experienced superintendents do not always recognize the importance of, as Collins (2001) said, getting "the right people on the bus." Others think about this but still make some poor choices. Here are several ways to avoid critical hiring mistakes.

Ensure That You Maintain Final Hiring Authority

It is important to invite others to participate in the hiring process. However, this does not mean delegating the actual hiring decision to them. For example, if you allow a group of teachers to select their own colleagues, would they be more likely to select someone who maintained the status quo or who helped move the school in a different direction? As superintendent, you should include others in the process but be careful to define their roles clearly. Most importantly, never relinquish administrative hiring authority.

Begin the Selection Process as Early as Possible

School districts are busy places. Because of the many day-to-day demands on administrators, there is almost always more to do than can be accomplished. As a result, you should expect that your administrators place a top priority on the hiring process. This includes beginning it as early as reasonable during the school year.

Broaden the Scope of Recruitment

After all is said and done, the only teacher and administrative candidates you will have to choose from are those who apply. If you have a small candidate pool, you limit your chances of employing a top performer. As superintendent, you want to ensure that the recruitment component of your selection process is extensive.

As our country's population grows in diversity, so too does the need for hiring a more diverse staff. As the new superintendent, you are in a strong position to take the lead on minority hiring. This begins with recruitment. You should not expect minority candidates to come to you.

If you want to attract highly qualified minority administrators and teachers, you must be an assertive recruiter. This means advertising vacancies in places minority candidates are most likely to see them. There are online job banks specifically serving teachers of color. In addition to the traditional recruitment strategies, you must ensure that your administrators establish contacts with universities and organizations that serve a diverse student body. Personal meetings with university placement officials can help to highlight your district as an attractive opportunity for potential candidates.

Emphasize Thoroughness

New superintendents can miss their best hiring opportunities by taking a path of least commitment. Some superintendents permit administrators to hire current teacher assistants, substitutes, or student teachers as new teachers without fully testing the employment market. Similarly, some superintendents select administrators merely because they are in the district. Even worse, some hire teachers and administrators because they are friends or relatives of school board members, superintendent colleagues, or other politically connected community members.

As a new superintendent, you must establish your employment expectations early. Others will observe how you manage your first selection process. Begin by expecting that all vacancies are filled only after a thorough selection process. Remember that you might receive lots of initial positive feedback because you hired a known or politically connected candidate. However, this decision may come back to haunt you if the person does not prove to be an excellent long-term employee.

Value Quality Over Convenience

As the new superintendent, you naturally want to be well liked. Who does not? Those who recommend teacher and administrative candidates are very pleased when their nominee is selected. This can be a win-win if the candidate selected is outstanding. However, when the person does not perform, making a convenient or popular hire may be one of the most significant personnel mistakes you can make.

If you hire someone who ultimately is not effective, the euphoria surrounding the initial choice will evaporate quickly. In the end, others will hold you responsible for the decision. For example, some superintendents hire principals who are not nearly as effective as others simply because the selection committee overwhelmingly supported the candidate. They assume that the committee will feel responsible for the decision. The truth is that committee members tend to have short memories. When future problems develop, remember that the "buck" never stops with the committee. They will hold you responsible.

As a new superintendent, you have to value quality over political convenience. This means that you might have to say no to a certain candidate even if you make some board members, administrators, teachers, or others unhappy. Over time, you will discover that it is always better to hire the strongest possible candidates. Their performance will easily overcome any initial consternation.

Provide Screening Interviews to Anyone Referred

One political mistake you want to avoid is ignoring referred candidates. It is always better to ensure that your administrators provide any referred candidates with at least a screening interview. Think how you would feel about neighboring superintendents if you called them to consider your daughter or son for a teaching vacancy and they never even contacted her or him.

An opportunity to interview does not equate with a job offer. On the other hand, you might be pleasantly surprised if a referred candidate turned out to be a strong teacher or administrator. If nothing else, you will earn the respect of others just for providing the opportunity.

Work with Your Board of Education Members So They Understand Your Role in the Hiring Process

Studies of teacher/administrator hiring practices have shown that, in a number of nonsuburban school districts, school boards still select administrators and teachers (Kersten 2008; Kersten 2006). As you can probably imagine, this can lead to any number of personnel problems. As a result, work with your board of education to convince them that this is one of your responsibilities. You may even want to clarify this during your board interview. A good compromise is to allow a board member or two to participate in some phase of the selection process for administrative positions.

However, if you are hired into a district where board members insist on interviewing one or more candidates, you need to honor their request. Over time as you earn their confidence, you may be in a stronger position to change this practice. Remember that discretion is sometimes more important than valor.

ESTABLISHING YOUR SELECTION PROCESS

As noted earlier, it is critical to your success to hire the best employees possible. The days of selecting someone based on a brief interview or two are long gone. Selection processes for administrators and teachers are now highly complex and inclusive. Given this evolution, what components should you build into your selection processes?

Hiring Building Administrators

No positions are more important to you as superintendent than those of the building administrators, especially principals. A poor clerical staff member or teacher can have some negative effect on the school. But the impact of an ineffective principal can be catastrophic. In fact, a poor choice can affect your personal success or even your job security.

As a result, you would be wise to develop a comprehensive principal selection process to help ensure that you employ the best principal possible. You can never be one hundred percent certain that the candidate you select will succeed. However, if you include the following steps in your selection process, you will increase your chances for a successful hire.

Step 1: Begin Informal Recruiting Even Before You Have an Opening

As a beginning superintendent, you may want to consider preparing a list of possible candidates even if you do not have an opening. That way, if an unexpected vacancy occurs, you will not find yourself scrambling for quality administrative candidates.

Here are several informal recruiting strategies you can use to accomplish this.

- Begin to identify current district teachers who you believe may have administrative potential. Look for opportunities to invite them to assume leadership roles in your district. You may even want to consider establishing a simple in-district administrative mentoring program.
- Ask your current administrators who they see as potential administrators.
- Have informal conversations with other superintendents about teachers and assistant principals they see as future administrators.
- Seek out others who have a special knack for hiring good leaders. You have probably met other administrators who were excellent judges of talent. Make an effort to ask them if they can recommend anyone.
- Establish relationships with local educational administration professors. Encourage them to identify talented students. They often get to know their students well, especially if they supervised them during their administrative internships.
- Attend township, county, and other professional meetings to scout for talent. As you interact with teachers, assistant principals, and others in quasi-administrative positions, take note of those who impress you.
- Never pass up an opportunity to meet a potential candidate who someone recommends. View this as a recruiting opportunity and not an infringement on your time.

By establishing and regularly expanding your potential applicant list, you will have a ready flow of candidates to contact should you have an opening.

Step 2: Make Use of Multiple Recruitment Approaches

Once you have an actual vacancy, the real work begins. You want to initiate the recruitment process as soon as possible. Simultaneously, you should plan to employ as many recruitment strategies as you can. Superintendents who rely only on advertising on their district websites or through county/state associations may never meet the best candidates available. These individuals will apply only if they know you have a vacancy. Beyond traditional postings, here are other approaches to consider.

- Make personal calls to other administrators in your area and ask them if they know someone they could recommend. In all likelihood, they will identify individuals in their districts as well as from the outside. Such a direct approach is more effective than email or mailed requests that might be ignored.
- Encourage other district employees to recommend candidates.
- Work with your technology personnel to advertise through social media. Many of today's candidates have grown up in the digital world and regularly research electronic media for administrative positions.

Step 3: Establish a Realistic Selection Timeline

The length of your selection process will, of course, depend on the time of the year when the vacancy occurs. However, you want to ensure that you allow enough time to recruit well. If you do not, you may never meet some strong candidates.

At the same time, do not make it so long that you lose candidates to other school districts. You should also ensure that your process is flexible enough to adjust your timeline should you find yourself in competition with another district for a particular candidate.

Step 4: Schedule Brief Prescreening Interviews with as Many Candidates as Possible

As you begin the interview process, think of it as a funnel. Early on, you want to meet as many candidates as you can. You never know who you might miss if you are overly selective too soon. Have you ever had the experience of thinking you know someone purely by reputation or after a brief encounter? Then, after you really get to know the person, you discover that the person is quite different. You should apply this same principle when hiring. It is possible that someone who did not stand out on his or her application may be a strong candidate.

A thorough interview process begins with many brief, even fifteen- to twenty-minute, screening interviews. Think about screening interviews you have conducted in the past. Did you need much more than a few minutes before you knew whether the candidate might be viable? Scheduling thirty- to sixty-minute screening interviews is very inefficient. Brief interviews provide you an opportunity to assess many candidates quickly and efficiently.

Screening interviews should be informal. Begin by describing the position and engaging candidates in a discussion about their interest. Your goal is merely to determine in the broadest sense if a candidate is viable. One word of caution you should consider. It is important to let candidates know that the interview will be brief, so they do not interpret it as a lack of interest in them.

Step 5: Conduct Administrative Team Interviews

Once you have identified some potential candidates, it is time to ratchet up the interview process. However, treat this part of the process as fluid. Rather than waiting until all viable candidates have been selected, consider inviting several to the district for interviews with some of your administrators. At the very least, you should include one of your assistant superintendents or principals. These more in-depth interviews should be approximately thirty minutes in length, which is sufficient time to probe candidates' knowledge in the field and their beliefs about leadership. This second-level interview will also allow you to develop a better sense of whether the candidate is a good personality fit for your team.

You may want to consider using a consensus model during this phase. Under this approach, no candidate moves to the next step unless all interviewers agree. The advantage of consensus is that it forces you and your team to think through candidates' qualifications more thoroughly. It also helps avoid making snap decisions based purely on an individual's personality.

The consensus model, though, may not be useful in all situations. If you inherit an administrative team without thoughtful, collaborative members, you may have to defer such an approach until you are able to employ more team-oriented administrators.

Step 6: Schedule Informal School Visits with Your Most Viable Candidates

As viable candidates emerge following the administrative-level interviews, consider conducting informal visits to their schools. This will allow you to see them in their natural settings. One process mistake superintendents make is scheduling site visits with the final candidate or two at the very end of the selection process. By that point, everyone in their district knows that they are close to leaving. Will you really learn much about the candidate from such a visit?

A better approach is to conduct site visits with the most viable candidates before selecting your finalists. Rather than conducting comprehensive site visits with interviews and meetings, ask candidates to provide you with a brief tour of their school. Encourage them to keep the purpose of the visit confidential. They can treat you as they would any other visiting administrator. Avoid interviewing any administrators, teachers, or support personnel. This less intrusive approach will allow you to develop a much better sense of candidates.

As you walk through their schools, observe how they interact with adults and children. Notice how others respond to them. This can say volumes about their leadership style. By what they choose to show you and the depth of information they provide, you will gain a much better sense of their instructional leadership knowledge and skills.

Step 7: Check References

By this point, you may believe you know the candidate reasonably well. However, further due diligence will either confirm your impressions or bring to light new information. Most superintendents routinely check the traditional reference sources such as past and current supervisors. You want to do this too. However, you may have difficulty getting completely objective comments from their references. On the other hand, if you really want to be thorough, spend some time on informal reference checking.

For example, when you call the candidate's school, you might reach an office staff member or even a custodian. This is an opportunity to ask them informally about how the school year is going or similar general-type questions. How they spontaneously respond may provide you with some unexpected insights into their school's leadership.

Also, as a school administrator, you probably already know many individuals in other school districts who could be informal references. Now is the time to tap these contacts. A few well-placed and maybe even off-the-record probes can be insightful. Remember that your goal during reference checking is to gather as much additional information as you can to ensure that the principal you are hiring is who you think he or she is.

Finally, document your reference checking. You should create a simple form on which you record who you contacted and when. Write notes that may include quotes summarizing what references say. If later a candidate is unsuccessful or information surfaces about prior unknown or controversial issues, you can demonstrate that you did your homework.

Step 8: Invite Semifinal Candidates for Committee Interviews

Once you have narrowed your candidate pool to a manageable number, now is the time to increase the visibility of your selection process. Over the past few weeks, you have identified possible district interview committee members. You want to ensure that those appointed reflect local expectations and represent key stakeholders.

Here are the representative groups who should normally be invited.

- District administrators

- School board members
- Teachers from the school with the opening
- Clerical staff
- Parent organizations
- Students, if at the high school level

By employing broad-based participation, you will see how candidates respond under pressure. You will also let others know that you value their perspectives. At the same time, you will build some initial level of support for the successful candidate.

Yet, wide representative involvement should not mean group selection. It is important to clarify from the beginning that the role of committee members is advisory. If you explain your rationale for their advisory role, others will generally accept your position. They will understand that, since you are responsible for the selection, you should be the one who makes it.

At the same time, your committee members' perceptions will be very important to your objective assessment of each candidate. They can influence your selection. For example, you might enter the interviews believing that a certain candidate is very viable, yet after observing committee members' responses, realize that you cannot move forward with this individual.

In preparation for committee interviews, develop a timeline for interview day. You should build in a committee member in-service session. You want to make sure that they understand the process thoroughly and are familiar with each candidate's qualifications.

During the in-service, you should clarify that they will not be voting for or against candidates. To help keep committee members focused on advising, consider using a candidate assessment form with just three questions:

- What do you see as the candidate's strengths?
- What potential concerns do you have?
- What additional information should we seek out about this candidate?

The last question allows you to remind committee members that they are seeing only a snapshot of the candidates. As superintendent, you will be the only person who observes candidates throughout the process. Also, because you will be following up with one or more candidates, you will be in the best position to explore any unresolved questions.

At the end of each interview, ask committee members to share their responses to the three questions. Try to avoid responding to their comments. Rather, take notes. You want to make sure you have reviewed this debriefing process during the committee orientation. In this way, you will be able to minimize debate among committee members and possible lobbying for certain candidates.

Step 9: Include a Tour of the School for each Finalist

Some individuals are gifted interviewees. They wow committees with their personal skills and charisma. This can make hiring somewhat of an art rather than an exact science. One way to judge candidates beyond the interview is to add a school tour component. You can learn even more about who each candidate really is through informal school walk-throughs.

Following the interview, arrange for one of your administrators to guide candidates through the school while classes are in session. Encourage faculty and staff members to interact with candidates. It is helpful to provide staff members with the identical rating form you gave committee members. You should encourage them to return completed forms to you if they have perceptions to share.

As part of the tour, ask the guide to identify what the candidates seem especially interested in. Have them watch how they interact with adults and students. Later that day, ask your administrative guide to share perceptions with you. Often this simple step will either confirm or call into question information you have gathered to date.

Step 10: Conduct Final Reference Checks

Now that you have seen candidates in multiple situations, spoken with references, and gathered others' perspectives, you are ready for your final reference checks. This is the time to follow up on some of the questions that emerged during the interview process. Try to keep an open mind about your leading candidate. This means listening closely to references' responses rather than viewing checks as a mere formality. The more objective you can be, the more you will learn about the finalists.

Step 11: Make Your Recommendation to the Board of Education

After you have completed the process and made your final selection, now is the time to prepare your candidate recommendation for your board of education. Begin by developing a brief board memo in which you summarize your recommendation. You might include comments about the candidate that emerged during interviews, reference checks, and the site visit. This will demonstrate the thoroughness of the process. Remember that board members will want to know why your selection stands out from the other candidates.

After preparing your memo, first discuss your recommendation with your board president whose support will facilitate a smooth board appointment. You would be wise to send the memo as a confidential document to all board members. This will help avoid any surprises at the board meeting. Also, since you included some other board members in the process, they, too, can lend credibility to the selection process and your recommendation.

Hiring Teachers

In addition to hiring high-performing building-level administrators, the selection of highly competent teachers is a must. Effective teachers are one of the most important factors in whether students have a quality educational experience. Their performance affects both the success of the school and ultimately you as superintendent.

As the superintendent, you will not personally conduct the district teacher selection process unless you are employed in a very small school district. However, it is important for you to establish process selection expectations. In too many school districts, the teacher selection process is ill defined and unfocused. Because of day-to-day demands, some administrators may postpone teacher selection until the school year ends. Others make their teacher selections without a high level of due diligence.

As the school superintendent, you must ensure that teacher selection is your school district's number one priority. Since every teacher hire is key, you want to make sure that your administrators do not shortcut any phase of the selection process. Remember that, with every person you hire, you leave your legacy. As a result, you never want future administrators asking: Why did the administration ever hire these teachers? As you move into your superintendency, commit to employing a comprehensive hiring process.

Mirror Parts of Your Principal Hiring Process

Any teacher selection process should mirror most of the recruiting strategies discussed above. However, for teachers your recruiting process should place increased emphasis on web recruiting and job fairs.

Web Recruiting   Teacher candidates today are much more likely to turn to the Internet for vacancy announcements. Traditional university vacancy newsletters have almost disappeared. Today, candidates begin their searches by seeking Internet postings on university, county, professional organization, and school district websites.

Some candidates may even target a select group of districts and check their websites regularly. As a result, you may even want to contact other districts in your area to ascertain their interest in creating a common website that includes links to each district's vacancies.

Another way to improve your district candidate pool is to ensure that openings are easy to find on your website. If you use an online application, make sure that it links efficiently to your website. Also, consider including positive information about student performance, salary schedules, class size averages, and per pupil spending. Such data can attract candidates.

Technology can increase recruiting efficiency. However, if not used well, technology can become a recruiting deterrent. Some districts have such extensive, time-consuming web-based application processes that candidates avoid them. You should ensure that yours is only as complex as needed to gather necessary information. A useful question you may want to discuss with your administrative team is, "How can we develop a simple, concise application process that encourages candidates to apply and gives us the information we need to identify quality candidates?" User-friendly processes always yield more candidates.

Job Fairs   As you recruit teachers, you should consider participating in job fairs. These can be a quick, efficient way to meet a large number of candidates in a relatively short period of time. They are especially useful for hard-to-fill vacancies such as certain bilingual teachers or other specialists.

At the same time, job fairs can be overwhelming for both administrators and candidates. With some preplanning, you can increase their usefulness as a recruiting tool. Listed below are ways to improve job fair recruiting.

- Select a district team to conduct interviews.
- Limit interviews to five minutes or less.
- Create a positive public information sheet about your school district to distribute.
- Train team members on what to ask, the qualifications and personal qualities to consider, and how to make a snap judgment.
- Do not be too discriminating. Try to identify a larger rather than a smaller pool of "yes" candidates. They can be screened later to narrow the candidate pool.
- Have written information available for candidates on how to complete the application process.
- Schedule a meeting with interview team members as soon as possible after the job fair to identify the most viable candidates.
- Make sure you target promising candidates even in areas where you presently do not have a vacancy. You never know when someone may submit a resignation.

Teacher Selection Process Strategies

As with your principal selection, you want to ensure that when you select teachers you include extensive recruitment approaches, a workable selection timeline, and multiple interviews with administrators and, if appropriate, with teachers. In addition, you might want to build in the following strategies to further improve your process.

Strategy 1: Include a Demonstration Teaching Component   As you design your selection process, an important step is to build in a demonstration teaching component. Have you ever hired teachers who you thought would be great only to discover they were not who you thought they were? Often these individuals are adept interviewers who talk a good game but lack the teaching skills to match. The demonstration teaching step lets you get a glimpse of how they may actually perform in the classroom.

After you have narrowed your search to one or two finalists, expect each to teach a lesson in the school with the vacancy. If at all possible, focus the demo lesson in the grade level or subject area of the vacancy. You may have to improvise during summer school periods by finding an alternative teaching setting. The only time demo teaching may not be possible is when no classes are in session.

By conducting the demo lesson in your district, you equalize the playing field for candidates. As a result, you will be able to make a more objective assessment of each. It can also provide you with valuable insights into candidates' natural teaching skills and their abilities to relate with students.

To maximize the effectiveness of the demonstration teaching component, consider the following.

- Allow candidates to meet with the teacher in whose room the demonstration lesson will take place.
- Provide candidates with the option to extend the regular teacher's lesson or bring in their own.
- Ensure that two or more administrators observe the candidate. They will be able to share perceptions afterwards.
- Utilize a clinical observation approach with preobservation and postobservation conferences. This will allow you to gauge a candidate's knowledge of best practices. It will also permit you to assess their self-evaluation skills.

Strategy 2: Employ a Consensus Approach   One approach some school districts have used successfully to improve the accuracy of teacher hiring decisions is a collaborative administrative team process (Kersten 2010). Under this model, all administrators who are responsible for supervising instruction are required to "sign off" on any candidate prior to employment. In large school districts, this can be modified to smaller collaborative administrative units since it is not feasible for everyone to participate.

Since the selection process includes multiple interviews and demonstration teaching, each administrator should be expected to participate in at least one step. If a single administrator votes "no" on any candidate at any point in the process, the candidate is eliminated. Of course, as part of the discussion, administrators must justify their votes. Although you might miss a strong candidate or two, you will also substantially reduce your number of hiring mistakes.

Strategy 3: Consider Staff Reactions from Informal Interaction   Another important source to consider is your support staff. Office receptionists and secretaries at both the district office and schools see candidates in more informal settings. How candidates interact with them speaks volumes about how they may treat other support staff if employed. You want to make sure you tap these individuals for their perceptions.

SUMMARY

This chapter examined the importance of employing highly competent administrators and teachers. The chapter began with a discussion of ways to minimize typical hiring mistakes that can impede the selection of the best candidates. Also discussed were specific selection process components that superintendents can consider as they employ administrators and teachers. Finally, special strategies were offered to enhance the teacher selection process.

NINE

Avoiding the Most Critical Leadership Mistakes

As you step into your first superintendency, you want to avoid as many land mines as possible. This, though, is easier said than done. Even if you were a very successful administrator, the world of the superintendent is different. Have you ever known administrators who were stellar assistant superintendents or principals but struggled as superintendents?

Sometimes these struggles are unavoidable. You may simply inherit a set of difficult problems from your predecessor. Other times, you can find yourself facing a series of unpredictable events. These are merely the realities of district leadership.

Yet, some issues are predictable. In fact, you can avoid certain critical superintendent leadership mistakes if you recognize and plan for them. This chapter will examine several pitfalls, which were identified during interviews with experienced superintendents, leaders of superintendent associations, and school attorneys. Each was asked what superintendents do or do not do that either builds or undermines their success.

HAVING TOO NARROW A KNOWLEDGE BASE

Consider for a moment the backgrounds of almost any successful organizational leader. They are individuals who come to their positions usually after many years of successful experience at multiple levels of their organizations. One of the reasons they rise to the top administrative rung is that they have a broader understanding of their overall organizations.

Superintendents, similar to other CEOs, are expected to be well versed in all aspects of their school district's operation. Originally, they may have been hired because of a particular expertise, such as knowledge of

83

curriculum and instruction or school finance. But, ultimately, the superintendents who are most successful today possess a holistic understanding of all aspects of their school districts.

Being either a curriculum or finance expert only is not always sufficient. Since superintendents are viewed as the public face of the organization, they must be articulate spokespersons on any number of issues. They must be well versed in all aspects of the district. In fact, they must be prepared to respond to almost anything that is directed to them at board meetings, including closed sessions. They must also be perceived as having a good handle on all phases of their districts, especially during community events and day-to-day interactions with stakeholders. In summary, a superintendent is expected to be a jack-of-all-trades.

This expectation does not mean that superintendents must be experts in every area. Rather, they must be reasonably well informed. As a corollary, they must possess the ability to learn what they do not know and demonstrate that knowledge. For example, when having a conversation with a board member about a property tax limitation law, they must understand it well enough to discuss it accurately and intelligently. Similarly, when student achievement results are flat or declining, they must be up-to-date on the latest trends and practices so they can lead school improvement planning. If they cannot, board members may begin to question their competency as district leaders.

As a new superintendent, the level of response expected from you will vary depending on the size of your district and the level of administrative support. If you are in a very small school district, the knowledge bar may be much higher than if you are in a larger system. In fact, if you speak with any small district superintendent, you will discover that they wear multiple hats. At any time, they may be asked to develop a plan to solve a budget deficit problem while simultaneously coming up with a plan to increase student achievement. In larger districts, superintendents are expected to be articulate on any number of issues but not necessarily the expert. They have the luxury of relying on administrative specialists to provide more detailed expertise.

As you move into your first superintendency, you would be well advised to self-assess your areas of strength and limitations in district operations. Key areas include student achievement assessment, curriculum and instruction, school improvement, personnel, special services, finance, facility management, transportation, and food service. Once you have identified those where you have limited knowledge, you should develop a plan to become more informed.

Here are some ways to accomplish this.

- Meet with others who have expertise in specified areas. For example, if you are weak in school finance, spend time on a regular basis with a school business official to develop a stronger working knowledge.

- Attend program area meetings as an observer. This may mean committing precious time in areas where your current district already has a specialist. For example, if you have a limited understanding of special education, make time to sit in on district- and school-level special education meetings. You will learn a great deal by being part of the conversation.
- Look for professional development opportunities targeted at topics of limited knowledge to you. For example, your AASA state affiliate may offer workshops for superintendents on a topic such as leading district-wide student achievement improvement efforts.

By being personally proactive, you can quickly broaden your knowledge base. This will also provide you with the information you need to respond intelligently to questions and issues in the profession. You will also gain the confidence of your school board by presenting yourself as an informed leader.

LACKING FINANCIAL CREDIBILITY

As the new superintendent, you must earn a reputation as credible district leader. Others need to believe that, when you say something, it is accurate. This includes being forthright when you are not sure about something. Credibility also means staying true to your word. When you are viewed as credible, you are challenged less and trusted more.

One of the most important areas in which to establish your credibility is in financial management. Board members, employees, and parents must see you as an accurate financial analyst. If you underplay or exaggerate the school district's financial position, you will lose the support and confidence of others.

Here are several financial practices by which to lead.

- Insist that all administrative team members report financial information as accurately as possible. Make sure that they never underestimate the severity of any negative district financial data. At first, providing a more positive interpretation of data may minimize conflict. However, when reality hits, you and your administrative team's credibility will be hurt. If your stakeholders do not believe what you say, will they trust you in the future?
- Admit when you do not have all the answers. A mistake some new superintendents make is providing either inaccurate or wrong answers to board members' financial questions. If you are asked at a board meeting, for example, to explain why some taxpayer property tax bills increased dramatically while others declined, make sure

you know why before responding. It is acceptable to tell school board members that you will research the topic and get back to them, as long as you do not do so too often. Such a response shows them that you are thoughtful and value accuracy over expediency.

- When preparing financial projections, be conservative. It is always better to slightly underestimate revenues and overestimate expenditures. The key word here is "slightly." You never want to project that the district is in a much better financial position than it actually is. You want your projections to be reasonably close. At the same time, you will be better received if the year-end financial report shows the district in a slightly stronger position. If your projections are too far off, your credibility as a financial manager will be called into question. As a result, do your financial planning homework. That is, study recent trends and current financial data before developing projections.

- Be cautious when deciding to make staffing reductions. Part of long-range financial planning is deciding when to reduce district positions. You might think that prudent superintendents would err on the side of reducing a large number of positions. However, staff reductions which are too extensive or unsupported by financial projections can impact your reputation and credibility.

For example, if you convince your school board that you are facing a potential financial crisis and recommend that they reduce staff, you should be absolutely confident in your assessment. If you are wrong and actually finish the year in a more stable position, the board and staff may perceive you to be an overreactor rather than a thoughtful planner. This will be especially true if the district experiences negative consequences, such as higher class sizes or the loss of some of your most effective staff members, because of your actions. Remember that staffing reductions stir up staff members while creating board and parent unrest. They also lead to a reduced focus on teaching and increased concerns for job security.

FAILING TO MAINTAIN CONTINUITY

When you step into your superintendency, focus first on continuity. At the same time, recognize that this may be situational. You may be requested by the board or required by district circumstances to be more proactive. Only you can ultimately make this call.

Put thoughts of substantial change on the back burner. Consider former administrators, including principals, you have known over the years. Did some make changes too quickly and either complicate their transitions or even eventually fail? In almost all instances, it is more effective to spend most of your first year assessing needs rather than focusing on immediate change. This is especially true if you follow a long-standing, popular superintendent.

MISREADING DISTRICT POLITICS

Another mistake beginning superintendents can make is failing to read critical political cues. One way to avoid this is to ensure you are not office-bound. Make it a practice to interact with other administrators, faculty, staff, parents, and community members to better understand what they are thinking and feeling. By doing this, you can also more accurately assess informal district priorities.

ASSUMING SHORT-TERM SECURITY

When you assume your superintendency, you should not expect that all board members who hired you will be there the following year. It is possible that some board supporters only remained on the board long enough to see through the superintendent search process. They may not have intended to stay beyond their current terms. Others will turn over naturally during the next board election.

As you move into your new position, you want to avoid putting on the job security blinders. As mentioned earlier, meet with each board member individually to get to know them and their interests as well as the talents they bring to the board. Do not assume that, because you are new, you are automatically protected for some period of time. Instead, become an astute assessor of board and community members' opinions and agendas. This does not mean developing job security paranoia. Rather, it implies assessing people and situations realistically but cautiously. Once you begin to develop your political radar, you will understand others better and be more adequately prepared to respond.

FAILING TO RECOGNIZE CHANGING LEADERSHIP NORMS

Not long ago, superintendents could go out for long lunches, which included a drink or two. Some were regular guests of vendors at elaborate golf outings often during the work day and, at times, extending over more than a day. Some were even held in vacation locations. Still others accepted lavish dinners, logo clothing, trips to sporting events, and concert tickets. You should recognize that, as Bob Dylan sang, "Times they are a-changin'." Today, depending upon where you are superintendent, accepting sizeable gifts can spell career disaster. In fact, some states, such as Illinois, have legal limits on acceptable gift types and amounts (Braun 2010).

As you weigh options, you must carefully consider the upside versus downside of any gifts offered. Ask yourself whether attending an expensive event sponsored by a potential vendor is worth the personal risk. A way to judge this is to think about what reaction you might receive from a typical taxpayer or board member if they knew you attended.

Similar to so many issues in public education, vendor or other sponsored events are never problems until someone makes them one. As you consider any potential "perk," ask yourself if you would be comfortable defending your attendance to a board or community member or worse yet a reporter after a district crisis occurred.

NOT RECOGNIZING ELECTRONIC COMMUNICATION TRAPS

As electronic communication becomes more and more prominent, superintendents need to be more aware of potential risks. There is no question that communication technology has increased the efficiency of district leadership. However, its overuse can have unintended negative consequences for you as a new superintendent.

Too often superintendents become lulled into complacency about their use of electronic communication. More and more, school attorneys are advising superintendents to avoid putting too much communication in any written form. They note that anything written including in an electronic format is a potential problem because these are considered public documents. Just as important, they can be forwarded to anyone at any time.

Electronic communication also increases documentation should you mistakenly include something you should not have. As a result, school attorneys advise superintendents to increase their face-to-face communication, especially when dealing with potentially sensitive matters. Only you can judge when something should be communicated only verbally. However, if you consider this issue before responding, you will minimize potential problems you may encounter later.

In addition to regular electronic communication, be cautious in your use of social media such as Facebook, YouTube, and Twitter. This is an area that is evolving rapidly. While you do not want to be left behind, you do not want to be on the bleeding edge. Use these with great caution. Remember that, in this media age, there is no such thing as "off the record."

MISHANDLING CRISES

Have you noted that, whenever a crisis erupts, one of the first questions asked is who knew what and when? The media is quick to single out leaders who had information on which they failed to act expeditiously. The government's response after Hurricane Katrina is a classic example of the type of slow leadership response that kicks off the blame game.

Although school district crises are not usually as far reaching as a hurricane disaster, they often place superintendents under similar scrutiny. As a new superintendent, you may find yourself faced with complex problems at an unexpected moment. Typical issues include a child's death, criminal use of technology, bullying, bomb threats, sexual harassment, or a weapon violation. The list, of course, is endless.

Before you find yourself in such a situation, you must prepare as well as you can. Here are several crisis management strategies to consider. Using them can help minimize some of the eventual fallout you might otherwise experience without proper planning.

Principle 1: Respond Quickly but not Hastily

As noted above, you must expect to be questioned about how long you knew about it before you responded. Whenever a significant problem occurs, do not attempt to convince yourself that it will disappear quietly. Consider the real possibility that someone will challenge your response time, possibly at a school board meeting.

On the other hand, you do not want to respond too hastily. If you do, you might exacerbate the situation. Although there is no definitive response timeframe for all situations, ask yourself this question. If you were to observe other superintendents facing a similar crisis, within what length of time would you expect them to respond? Your answer will help guide you.

Principle 2: Do Not Leave Crisis Management to Chance

Preparing for potential crises is a must. Although you cannot fully plan for all crises, you should prepare as thoroughly as possible. This begins with recognizing that, when a crisis occurs, you will be questioned about whether you had district policies and procedures in place. Consider for a moment the Katrina example. After the hurricane struck, those in leadership positions were put on the spot by various reporters and other politicians to show their disaster plans. What emerged were television images of leaders stumbling through their responses because they were not well prepared.

As a new superintendent, you want to work with your administrative team and others, such as social workers or public relations staff, to ensure that you have emergency management plans in place to respond to as many potential crises as possible. You also want to ensure that your district staff members are familiar with them and prepared to respond appropriately. Remember that the time to develop emergency evacuation procedures, including alternative student housing locations, is before there is a bomb threat, not during it. You want to be able to show the board and community that you are well prepared for crises.

Principle 3: Place a Premium on Student and Staff Safety

No matter what, always emphasize student and staff safety and not administrative convenience. Avoid any tendency to minimize any issues because you know they will be uncomfortable for you as the superintendent. You must accept the reality that the superintendency is fraught with discomfort.

Consider for a moment recent media reports about administrators who were informed about student bullying but failed to act. Think about instances of student sexual abuse that were never reported to the proper authorities by administrators but later became public knowledge. Although dealing with these when they occur is controversial, responding to them months or even years later is far worse.

As the new superintendent, you set expectations for others. As part of this, you must expect quick and thorough responses from all district employees. If you place the safety of children and adults as the number one priority, you cannot go wrong.

Principle 4: Respect Confidentiality

When any problem rises to the level of the superintendent, it is usually fairly substantial. Many times these are people issues that require increased confidentiality. For example, you might have parents make an appointment with you to discuss the enrollment of their child with AIDS. You might also have a faculty member approach you to file a sexual harassment complaint.

These are the types of complex problems you could face. Each is complicated by confidentiality requirements. How well you respond to them can be a key to your personal success. As the new superintendent, you should call a school district attorney for counsel. Too much internal administrative district discussion could lead to breaks in confidentiality that could call into question your judgment.

Principle 5: Provide Timely Superintendent–Board Communication

Board members never appreciate surprises. A quick way to undermine their confidence in you is to fail to recognize when you must share information with them. What can complicate this are the consequences of sharing too much information. Overcommunication can lead to board member micromanagement and/or breach of confidentiality.

In deciding whether you need to inform your board members about an issue, first weigh the extent of informal conversation both in and outside the district. That is, consider what you are hearing in the schools and community. If parents are talking about something or staff members are stirring, you can be pretty well assured that board members will hear this.

In these instances, it is better to be a proactive communicator. When you take the initiative to inform the board, you control the message. Depending upon the intensity of the issue, simply including a memo with your board meeting packet may be sufficient. Remember, though, that it is best to provide only the minimum amount of information needed and, if appropriate, actions you have taken or have planned.

If the anticipated reaction is more far reaching, a special board memo or even call to individual board members may be warranted. In any event, timely, objective communication will be well received. In the process, you will also communicate to board members that you are on top of district activities.

SUMMARY

Avoiding critical leadership mistakes is important to your early success. This chapter included a discussion of common mistakes that superintendents can make to undermine their success. Also discussed was the importance of ensuring that you develop a good basic understanding of all aspects of the district. In addition, this chapter examined ways to earn financial credibility, maintain district continuity, and read the political environment. Finally, the risks associated with electronic communication, the importance of appropriate crisis response, and use of timely board communication were explored.

TEN

Managing School District Financial Resources

In a recent study of educational leadership programs, superintendents were asked what knowledge and skills are most critical for inclusion in superintendent preparation programs. Overwhelmingly, respondents identified knowledge of school finance as number one (Hunt et al. 2011). In this day when the discussion of student achievement and school improvement dominates so much of the public education discussion, why is it that superintendents first mention school finance?

The answer is actually quite simple. Without adequate resources and solid fiscal management, school leaders and their staffs cannot focus fully on teaching and learning. In fact, when school districts lack financial stability, teachers and principals become increasingly more concerned about operational and job security issues than improving student learning. As a result, instead of school conversations focusing on what is taught, instructional methodology, and student performance, suddenly employee welfare takes center stage.

In addition, superintendents today feel great pressure to "keep the ship afloat." When the district conversation shifts from program improvement to financial constraints, superintendents suddenly find themselves in the center of a potential maelstrom. On the one hand, those who have little direct connection with the school district preach fiscal conservativeness. Comments such as "When I was in school, we did just fine without all these new programs and services" are common. On the other hand, teachers and parents typically ask for even more programs and services. They tend to be "now" focused. Seldom do they consider the long-term implications of reducing class size or expanded employee salaries and benefits.

As the new superintendent, you will walk into a district on any point in the financial spectrum from a solid financial position to financial distress. How well you respond to constituents and the district financial circumstances will impact your success.

DEFINING YOUR FINANCIAL PHILOSOPHY

One of the worst mistakes you can make as you assume your first superintendency is to fail to define your personal financial philosophy. If you do not, you will present yourself as unsure and maybe even rudderless. Unless others understand your financial management philosophy, they will be more reticent about following your leadership. Whether they agree with it or not will be less important than a lack of clarity. To help avoid putting yourself in an overreactive position, be prepared to articulate what you believe about school district fiscal management. Otherwise, your school board may perceive you to be a weak leader.

The time to come to grips with what you believe about school district financial management is prior to even interviewing for a position. You can be assured that you will be quizzed about school finance throughout the superintendent interview process. As a result, it is imperative that you develop a working knowledge of school finance and define a set of financial management principles by which you will intend to operate.

Begin by recognizing that public school finance systems are state-specific. As a result, you should focus on understanding how schools are funded in your state. As part of this, you need to have a working knowledge of school finance–related issues so you can be an informed spokesperson. Here are some questions to consider.

- What are the primary sources of public school revenue in your state?
- How is each revenue source structured?
- Who has the primary authority for funding schools state-wide?
- Do public schools operate under any type of property tax restrictions?
- What are the board's borrowing authority limits for operations and capital improvements?
- How do the state legislature, local school boards, and voters impact the state school funding system?
- What are the unique provisions either included or not included in your state constitution related to school funding?
- What are the legal requirements for collective bargaining and unionization?
- In the event of inadequate revenues, what options would be available to you to increase your state funding?

Once you have a better sense of school funding in your state, you will be in a position to begin to define your personal financial management philosophy. Here are some principles of fiscal management you may want to consider.

Principle 1: Err on the Side of Conservativeness

The time to communicate that you are a conservative fiscal leader is from the day you first interview. You can begin by letting anyone you meet know that you value long-term financial stability over short-term expediency. This means telling others that your natural tendency is to maintain as strong an educational program as possible within the constraints of the district's financial position. By doing so, you let your school board members know where you stand. That way, they will be more likely to support you should you resist popular but unwise expenditure requests in the future.

Principle 2: Be Wary of Adding Ongoing Costs

An important financial management principle is recognizing the difference between one-time and ongoing costs. There is a substantial difference between adding a new program or an additional teacher versus a one-time facility project. Think long and hard before you decide to add any annual costs that increase year after year. Also, ongoing costs such as staffing and program additions are often difficult to eliminate once they are approved. If your school district either has lower reserves or is trending toward deficit, it is better to say "no" upfront than find yourself in the position of "cutter" later.

Principle 3: Hire Nearer the Beginning Steps of the Salary Schedule

The one time you have real control over salary costs is when you have employee turnover. Even if overall board costs for district salaries increase due to normal operations, you might still be able to lower your year-to-year overall salary costs by limiting incoming employee pay. Since salaries costs compound over time, the greater the differential between those leaving and their replacements, the more positive the financial impact over time.

In some districts, boards of education want input into this hiring strategy. If yours does, you should have a philosophical discussion with your board during which you agree to a level or range of experience for which you will pay. As part of this discussion, you should provide the board with a detailed analysis of the long-term impact of hiring employees at various experience levels. If at all possible, avoid establishing a formal board hiring policy. This may prove too restrictive later. Recommended employment guidelines under which your administrators manage the hiring process are preferable. Also, if at all possible, avoid including hiring requirements in collective bargaining agreements.

Principal 4: Balance Additions with Reductions

An important financial management principle to consider is addition and reduction. That is, whenever you plan to add a position or program not linked to a student enrollment increase, try to offset the costs by reducing somewhere else. Principals and other district employees can be quick to increase staffing. From their perspective, these increases improve educational programs and services. They do not naturally consider the long-term impact of increased expenditures. By stressing the principle of paying for additions with offsetting reductions with your administrators and other staff members, you are more likely to ingrain this type of thinking into the district culture.

Principle 5: Look for Regular Opportunities to Be More Efficient

It is easy to be complacent when not facing major financial crises. However, that is actually the best time to look for cost savings. For example, rather than accepting current premium costs for health, liability, and property casualty insurances, you should explore your options. By soliciting quotes or bids, you may be able to reduce ongoing costs. In fact, by even suggesting a bidding process, you may be able to force your current providers to sharpen their pencils.

You might also approach your employee groups about studying ways to lower costs for both them and the board. Sometimes minor adjustments in employee insurance coverage such as prescription co-pays can result in significantly lower premium costs. You might explore the feasibility of a Health Reimbursement Account (HRA). Through an HRA, employees receive a specified dollar amount from the district that they can use to offset medical expenses such as increased health insurance deductibles and co-pays. In exchange, employees agree to increase their deductibles, which substantially lowers premiums for them and the school district, a win–win for the employees and board.

Principle 6: Be Careful How You Use Competitive Grant Funding

Competitive grants can be an important source of revenue, especially in school districts with special needs student populations. Grants may also be a welcome source of revenue for districts with financial issues. However, it is important to remember that they are most useful for non-recurring expenditures such as instructional materials, equipment, or capital improvements.

When school districts experience revenue shortfalls, one of the first suggestions you hear from board members is to look for competitive grants. It is common for them to assume that there are substantial grant dollars available for the taking. All that the administration needs to do is seek them out.

While these grants may provide opportunities for the district, they can be a drain on school resources. As superintendent, you will need to educate your board members and possibly even staff on the downside of competitive grants. First, remember that applying for grants for the sake of doing so is not educationally or financially prudent. Only seek grants that are tied to district and school priorities. Second, if grants are used to fund recurring expenditures such as staffing or consumables, you should plan for what happens to the program once grant funding is no longer available. One option is to reduce or eliminate grant-funded programs, which can create controversy. Another choice is to continue to fund services with district revenues.

Think long and hard before you decide to apply for any competitive grant to make sure the benefits outweigh the possible commitment of district funds to support the program.

FINANCIAL PLANNING

No matter what size your school district, financial planning is a key element of any plan to manage school district resources efficiently and effectively. Before you begin your superintendency, you should spend some time with the outgoing superintendent and, if the district has one, the school business official to review their multiyear projection model. Any experienced superintendent will attest to the importance of assessing the long-term financial position of the school district on a regular basis. A failure to do so can be a recipe for disaster. If you focus only on the district's current financial position, you increase the likelihood of underestimating the long-term impact of program changes. You will also lose important opportunities to make financial adjustments early enough to avoid future crisis.

Building Financial Projections

Before beginning the financial planning process, you must identify the software you will use to create your financial projections. You should first consider the software presently in use in the school district. Since financial planning is a common element of effective school district management, you may have a good system already in place. However, if you discover that the district either does not use financial projections or that the software is inadequate, you should consider other options. Superintendent colleagues can be very helpful in this area. Also, some state boards of education, such as Illinois, have financial planning services available, including projection software. Finally, commercial financial management firms also provide this service but often at a significant cost.

No matter what approach you use, building financial projections begins by making revenue and expenditure assumptions that are as accurate as possible. Consider for a moment if you were assessing the efficacy of purchasing a new home. Would you just look at your current income and expenditure levels to decide if you could afford it? Not likely. You would ask yourself questions such as these.

- How stable is my employment?
- Do I anticipate a change in my income level over the next few years?
- Will I face any large expenditure, such as my children's college tuition, in the near future?
- Do I have enough income to pay the mortgage and taxes if my spouse lost his or her job?

In short, you look out over several years to help you decide if you are comfortable adding new debt. You must also have enough confidence to know that you can live an acceptable lifestyle once you have purchased your new home.

The process is not a lot different when planning for your school district's financial future. First, you must do your homework. You must make informed judgments about what is likely to occur over the next five years on the revenue and expenditure sides of the financial equation. To do so, you need to review financial data from the past three or four years. Often past trends are a good indicator of the future. In addition, study what is happening at the state and local levels to help you predict where revenues and expenditures may be headed. You should include collective bargaining agreements as well as your best prediction regarding future contract negotiations.

Once you have finalized your assumptions, you are ready to prepare your basic multiyear projection. If your assumptions are accurate, your projections will be valuable. However, if you project revenues too high or expenditures too low, the results may prove unpleasant. You can lose credibility. You never want to be in a position where you have to tell your board of education that the district is in worse financial shape than you predicted. It is far better to announce that you ended the year in a more solid financial position.

Using the Financial Projection Process Strategically

Once you complete your basic financial projection, you have taken the first step toward managing your school district resources well. You are ready to use projections as a financial planning tool. By identifying strategies to increase revenues and reduce expenditures, you can test the impact of your actions against the bottom line before making any formal recommending. You can even use them to demonstrate to your board how failing to maximize revenues now can lead to financial crisis much sooner than they might think.

A key financial planning concept to remember is that the earlier you make a change in revenues or expenditures, the greater its future impact on the long-range financial position of the district. This is because of the compounding factor. One way to appreciate the compounding effect is to hypothetically either increase revenues this year or reduce expenditures in your projection model. If you look at the first year, the impact will be small. However, if you look out five years, you will see a dramatic effect.

As a new superintendent, vary your assumptions and study the impact on your multiyear projections. This is an effective way to help decide what actions to recommend to your board. By using projections effectively, you also demonstrate your financial planning acumen, which board members, especially from the business sector, will appreciate.

Presenting Financial Projections to the Board of Education

Financial projections are often presented to the school board or a board finance committee in conjunction with a discussion of sources of revenue such as the property tax levy. They can be an effective tool in helping even your most fiscally conservative board members realize the importance of maximizing revenues. At a time when the national economy is floundering and board members are becoming more fiscally conservative, you may find it more difficult to convince some board members to levy fully. However, through the use of financial projections, you have a tool with which you can demonstrate the negative effects that underlevying can have on long-term financial stability.

When presenting your financial projections to the board, you should also view this as an opportunity to educate your board as to the complexity of district leadership. As a result, you should plan on making as thorough a presentation as possible, especially during the first year in your superintendency. As part of your board report, you want to emphasize the following points.

- Financial projections are just that, projections. As such, they are your best estimate of the district's financial future. You want to point out that they are usually relatively accurate for only a couple of years. Be careful not to oversell.
- In addition to explaining the revenue and expenditure assumptions, identify as many unknown factors as possible. These include such items as pending state legislation, political initiatives, or social phenomena that might impact school funding in your state or even district. A classic example of a social change that dramatically impacted school finances was the introduction of birth control in the

late 1960s. Prior to its widespread use, student enrollments were booming and schools were being built rapidly. In less than a decade, a lower birthrate led to a sharp decline in school-age children. Remember that by highlighting potential unknowns you reinforce that projections are estimates.

- Link your projections to your levy recommendation or corresponding school board actions on revenues. Financial projections can serve to document current and future needs more objectively because they are data driven. It is much easier to convince board members to vote for a specific levy or other revenue income if you show how it impacts educational programs and services.

Updating Projections

Once you have presented your projections, you are only partially there. Good fiscal management requires ongoing financial monitoring. Although you will usually present projections annually to your board of education, you must continuously monitor your district's financial data. As revenue and expenditure information solidifies and new information emerges, you want to ensure you do the following.

First, revise your projections internally. By keeping a close watch on the district's position, you will be more prepared to answer any questions that arise during the normal course of business. Also, if something occurs that may have a substantial impact on your district, you will more likely find yourself on top of the situation.

Second, keep the board informed about any significant changes that may affect your district's financial health. You can rarely go wrong by alerting board members to emerging issues at the federal, state, or local levels that are either stirring politically or likely to become reality. You never want the board to be surprised, especially when you could have avoided it.

OTHER FINANCIAL REPORTS

In addition to financial planning, you should familiarize yourself with other ongoing financial reports that are typically prepared on a monthly or other regular basis for the board of education. These include approval of district bills, a summary of the school district's financial position, and financial investment updates. In addition, you should review reporting requirements that are unique to your state to ensure that you meet them. Also, make sure that you are aware of any additional reports that your board of education is accustomed to receiving. Attention to these will smooth your transition into the district.

SUMMARY

Chapter 10 focused on the superintendent's role in managing school district financial resources. It began with a discussion of the important role school finance plays in the day-to-day operation of the school district as well as the success of the superintendent. Explored also was the need for new superintendents to define a personal financial philosophy. This included key questions they should ask themselves, as well as sound financial principles to consider.

The importance of long-range financial planning was also noted. Suggestions were offered on how to build financial projections and use them strategically as the district leader. Ideas were offered on ways to present financial projections to members of the board of education while earning their trust and confidence. Finally, the value of updating projections regularly was emphasized.

ELEVEN

Working Smarter, Not Harder

The superintendency is perhaps the busiest and most demanding position in education. As a result, it should come as no surprise that most beginning superintendents experience work overload. From the first day on the job, they start to learn just how much they must do and how little time they have to accomplish it. Such expectations can create a great deal of personal pressure and performance uncertainty.

What can complicate this career transition further are the personal strengths and weaknesses that new superintendents bring to their positions. Consider for a moment administrators you have known during your career. Were not some highly focused and extremely well organized while others approached their responsibilities more globally? Did some view most issues from a black or white perspective while others tended to see shades of gray?

Although no one particular skill set is always preferable, certain ones are more associated with success than others. Administrators who are on top of the details, meet deadlines, and are timely tend to be viewed as efficient and effective. Rarely do they appear to "fly by the seat of their pants." They also tend to have an increased ability to work well with a broad spectrum of personalities.

As you approach the superintendency, you would be well served to ensure that you understand your personal strengths and weakness. If you do, you will be better prepared to capitalize on your strengths and accommodate any weaknesses. A good starting point is to consider the work of Myers and Briggs (Myers and Briggs Foundation 2010).

MYERS AND BRIGGS

Back in 1962, Katharine Cook Briggs and her daughter Isabel Briggs Myers developed the Myers-Briggs Type Indicator instrument based on the research of Carl Jung. The assessment tool was designed to identify personality preferences along four continua: extrovert (E)–introvert (I); sensing (S)–intuition (N); thinking (T)–feeling (F); and judging (J)–perceiving (P) (Myers and Briggs Foundation 2010).

Myers-Briggs developed a forced-choice response questionnaire that you can use to identify your key personality preferences. For example, you can assess whether you tend to be more of an extrovert (E) rather than an introvert (I), and whether your tendency is to take in information through your senses (S) or are more "big picture" (I) focused. You can also identify whether you see the world from a spontaneous, open-ended, flexible perspective (P) or tend to favor more organization, structure, and closure (J). Finally, you can determine whether you tend to be a cognitive-analytical decision-maker (T) or one who relies more on feelings (F). Neither is necessarily good or bad; they are just different (Briggs Myers 1993).

By taking the Myers-Briggs instrument, which includes the instrument and scoring guidelines and is available either online or in print, you will better understand your personal tendencies. You will also begin to appreciate the different tendencies of those with whom you interact. Once you do, you will be able to play to your strengths while better understanding why others do what they do. You will, in turn, find yourself better positioned to appreciate why others respond to you as they do. Finally, through the Myers-Briggs self-assessment, you can identify those areas for your personal development especially related to success in the superintendency.

In addition to using it personally, you might ask your district's administrative staff members to complete the instrument as part of your professional administrative development program. In this way, your administrative team members, too, can gain valuable insights into their own personality preferences. Then, as a team, you will better understand each other and capitalize on the strengths of your individual team members. However, you should wait to do so until you have developed a level of trust with them. If not, they may be suspicious of your intentions and less open to a real discussion.

STRATEGIES TO WORK SMARTER, NOT HARDER

No matter how well organized and detailed you are, increasing your personal efficiency will contribute to your success as a superintendent. This will be even more important in the future as the demands and complexity of district leadership increase. Below are several recommended strategies that can help you work smarter, not harder.

Strategy 1: Minimize Time Spent on Mail Management

One of the most significant time-wasters is mail management. Because superintendents are the top district decision-makers, those inside and outside the school district either want to get their attention or be a fixture on their radar. They know that, if the superintendent supports something, the likelihood of it happening is dramatically increased. As a result, superintendents often find themselves inundated with both useful and useless mail daily. If they go to their district mailboxes, chances are that the mail is piled quite high.

As a new superintendent, if you allow the mail to accumulate, before long you will have a huge stack with which to contend. As it grows, it will begin to weigh on your mind, which may affect your efficiency. One way to manage your mail and minimize the time you spend reviewing it is to delegate to one of your office staff members the responsibility for presorting it. With clear guidance from you, staff can be trained to distribute it to the appropriate administrator or staff member. Also, they can eliminate any "junk" mail before handing the remainder of the mail to you.

If you do delegate mail review, you can run the risk of missing some important items. However, over a relatively short period of time, you will be able to ascertain whether this is an issue. In the meantime, you might ask them to let you make the decision on any mail item about which they have any questions.

When your mail arrives at your desk, you can increase your personal efficiency through a simple act. Stand next to the garbage can and make a snap decision about discarding items before opening them. In most instances, you will not miss them. However, for some superintendents, this strategy can be difficult. They feel the urge to look at each item. However, if you get into the habit of culling your mail immediately, you will soon discover that you can free up to at least fifteen minutes in your daily routine while decreasing office clutter.

In addition to traditional paper-based mail, another type is email, the use of which can increase or decrease your efficiency. As a new superintendent, you must recognize when email becomes more of a time trap than timesaver. One classic misuse is participating in humorous email exchanges among groups of individuals. While these may be entertaining, they waste a great deal of work time while drawing others into participation to feel part of the group.

You should also ask yourself if you need to respond to every email sent from others. Although it is common courtesy to let someone know you received their message, where do you draw the line when responding back and forth? Do you thank them for thanking you? You will need to decide just how you can minimize these types of email communication. If you do, you will minimize the unnecessary use of time for both you and others.

Another time savings approach is to take Reply All from your repertoire. Some administrators overuse the Reply All button, which creates unnecessary, time-consuming communication. In fact, even merely deleting all these emails takes time. As the district leader, you can increase the efficiency of your entire staff by expecting others to minimize the use of Reply All. Maybe just as important, you also reduce the chances of you or one of your staff responding Reply All to something that creates a problem.

It is equally important to identify how you configure your district email system to increase and not limit employee efficiency. As the superintendent, you should ensure that your district takes full use of the "junk mail" or similar features. If certain emails never reach you or other employees, you do not need to respond to them. Even this simple step improves efficiency. Yes, you might have an important email blocked. However, the risk–reward of email filtering favors its use.

Finally, become a "delete junkie." For some administrators, hitting the delete button is difficult. Rather than dealing with emails immediately, they leave them sitting in their inbox, intending to get back to them later. Such an approach leads to email screen overload, screen after screen of emails left on hold. It also creates electronic clutter while making you feel a sense of personal inefficiency.

Others go even further. They start to create email subfolders in which they park emails. This is not much different from saving hard copies of everything on the off chance that you may need them someday. Administrators who do this often have cluttered files and papers stacked in their offices. Undeleted emails are the electronic version of paper stacking.

To avoid email hoarding and to increase personal efficiency, consider the following ways to approach email communication.

- Get in the habit of deleting. Whenever you log on to your computer, review each unopened email and delete as many as you can before opening any. This way you will not get bogged down reading unnecessary emails. As advertisers have increased email marketing, daily junk mail sometimes exceeds regular email. For example, rather than reading emails from groups with which you have no connection, such as those advertising international conferences, delete these immediately if you know you have no interest. Once you get in the delete habit, you will feel good about your newfound efficiency.
- Avoid the temptation to be an email junkie. Some administrators cannot resist checking their inbox every few minutes. If you do, you

will waste valuable time. Very few messages are so critical that you must watch for them continuously. Rather, set specific times to check email. For example, you might check it each hour. It is also helpful to turn off the new email notification. If you do not, you may find yourself drawn to your computer too often. If email checking is really a problem, avoid having your email page up on your screen. This will further limit the temptation.

- Keep personal email separate from your district email. This will avoid the appearance of using work time for personal business. Also, remember that your district email is subject to Freedom of Information Act requests.

- Create a subfolder called File Cabinet. Some emails must be saved. For example, as superintendent, you will receive emails about parent or board issues as well as employee problems that you may need to make use of at a later date. Rather than letting them accumulate in your Inbox, move them to your File Cabinet. That way, you will be able to minimize the number of current email screens without losing potential future documentation.

- Select one day a year, preferably during a slow vacation period, to review and delete Archived emails. If you fail to review these at some regular point, your Archive folder will become overloaded.

- Take a few minutes before you leave your office each Friday to clean out your "In" and "Sent" boxes. The most efficient way to do this is through the "Received" option. Clustered emails are easier to review than those organized by date received.

- Ensure that your email system is set up to automatically clean your delete box regularly.

- Check your email account sometime on Sunday evening with the intent of deleting all unnecessary emails. The reality today is that the five-day, eight-hour work week is no longer viable. Most administrators cannot refrain from checking emails at any time of the day. Since you will likely do so, you will feel better about yourself if you delete as many unimportant emails as possible on Sunday night. That way, when you arrive at the office on Monday, you will start your week with a screen of reduced emails. This will give you a psychological and organizational boost as you begin your week.

- Make time to "unsubscribe." As the volume of advertising emails, especially daily ones, increases, you should spend some time unsubscribing. For example, do you receive emails from unfamiliar organizations or commercial advertisers? You would save time overall by taking time to unsubscribe now. You might even consider asking a trusted office staff member to do this for you.

Strategy 2: Keep Emails Brief

Email should be used for short, brief communications. If you have complicated information to communicate or something sensitive, consider another form of communication.

Strategy 3: Maximize Electronic Communication Efficiency

As much as electronic communication has improved management efficiency, if not used well, it can have the opposite effect. How often in your career have you found yourself in the middle of email or phone "tag"? Here is where technology can save you and others valuable time. For example, web-based software today is available to help you manage meeting scheduling more efficiently. For example, you could use software, such as Doodle, to schedule meetings quickly and more efficiently. After creating an online calendar of possible meeting dates and times, participants are asked to indicate on which dates they are available. You and other meeting participants can quickly see who is available and when.

These types of technology-driven solutions abound. The problem is finding and evaluating their effectiveness for your individual situation. One way to accomplish this is to identify technology support specialists or other administrators you know who tend to be particularly tech savvy. They can be an invaluable technology resource. Not only can they tell you what is available, but they can advise you on its use. These individuals may also be helpful in recommending public and private sector workshops and seminars that you would find useful in order to avoid attendance at sessions of limited value.

Another time trap is website searching. Because these are so readily accessible, some administrators spend entirely too much precious time visiting extraneous websites. As the new superintendent, you may want to let others know that you view this type of activity as inappropriate.

While electronic communication can be very beneficial, its use can also contribute to increased personal inefficiency. Using technology just because it is considered in vogue encourages inefficiency. In fact, some administrators have become so glued to their desk chairs that they spend entire days sitting at their computers. Although using technology can create the impression of focused work, unfortunately, just working at a computer does not equate with productive work time. You should measure your productivity by what you accomplish rather than the amount of time at the computer.

Strategy 4: Minimize Your Use of Unnecessary Paper

In addition to managing electronic communications, some administrators deal inefficiently with paper documents. Superintendents, similar to the general public, have different personality styles as evidenced by Myers and Briggs (2010). Some just cannot make the decision to throw away unnecessary paper. Some will always try to justify their cluttered offices by saying that they can put their finger on any document at any time. Whether this is true or not, clutter leads to a waste of time and creates the appearance of disorganization.

If you tend to be a saver, you may want to consider the following suggestions.

- Try not to touch any piece of paper more than once. Although it is easy to say, it is often difficult to do. However, the more you can practice this strategy, the greater the likelihood that you will be able to discard unnecessary documents.
- Try to maximize your open desktop space. Once you begin to place a priority on ensuring that a certain portion of your desktop is always visible, the easier it will be to train yourself to be more efficient.
- Avoid the temptation to add file cabinets or other storage spaces to your office. If they are not there, you will be more likely to cull through written documents rather than save them.
- Ask yourself if you really need more than a single copy of any written document. Inefficient administrators regularly make more than one copy of almost everything. By minimizing excessive copying, this will become more automatic.
- Think green. Convince yourself that fewer copies save time, money, and the environment. By setting this as a district priority, you will be more likely to lead by example.
- Avoid printing emails if at all possible.

Strategy 5: Create a Personal Planning Calendar

As a new superintendent, it is important to put your arms around the major organizational tasks, regular meetings, important deadlines, and district and school activities for the upcoming year as soon as possible. To accomplish this, begin by creating a month-by-month calendar in which you list each. As you do, pay special attention to time-sensitive deadlines to ensure you include them.

As you begin this process, start by reviewing past board meeting agendas and minutes. These will include board actions on key items. In addition, consult with your administrative assistant who can review your draft calendar and offer additional items. Similarly, rely on your administrative staff, especially school business officials and curriculum directors, who are very knowledgeable in their respective areas. After you finalize your draft calendar, you would be wise to ask an experienced superintendent to review it also. Such planning will ensure you never miss important deadlines such as filing your tax levy or riffing a teacher.

Strategy 6: Plan to Maximize Your Daily Use of Time

A great challenge for some superintendents is maximizing their day-to-day efficiency. Because there is so much to do and such a high level of personal interaction, it is easy to become distracted from the task at hand. If, for example, you begin a task and then shift to another without seeing the first through, you will find yourself wasting time. Your inefficiency will be further exacerbated if this shift requires moving from one work place to another. On the other hand, with more upfront planning, you can make better use of your available time.

If you are time-management challenged, you might want to consider the following suggestions.

- Streamline your day by either arriving early or staying late to focus on non–time sensitive tasks. What time during the day you choose to do this depends on whether you tend to be a morning or an afternoon person. Because most other employees are not at work, you will find that you have uninterrupted time to focus on what you need to do. You also can avoid the "Do you have a minute?" interruptions that often force you to stop and restart tasks and affect efficiency. This time is best used to write reports, develop plans, and complete paperwork that requires focused attention for some extended period of time.
- Prioritize what you know you need to address during the day. Although you will have many unexpected interruptions, you should plan well for expected tasks. Begin by listing the tasks you need to complete. Afterward, prioritize each into high and low categories. Once you do, this will save you time because you will be focused on what needs to get done rather than revisiting tasks over and over during the day. At the same time, you can adjust your list if needed as new priorities emerge.
- Do not procrastinate on those tasks you find unpleasant or have less interest in doing. Convince yourself that you need to respond to all your high priorities. If you continue to avoid the less pleasant ones, you will waste time and energy by revisiting them over and over during the day. At the same time, you will feel a sense of accomplishment when they are completed.
- Consider closing your office door for some time during the day. As long as you do not do so for long periods or too often, this is a good way to limit interruptions and give yourself time to focus on something specific. Consider varying the time of day, length, and frequency. If you do, you should also let others know that you will periodically close your door and your rationale for doing so. That way, others will not wonder what you are doing behind closed doors.

- Increase your level of delegation. Some of the most inefficient administrators are those who have to do everything themselves. Provide others the authority to take leadership and make them the decision-makers for as many tasks as appropriate. Not only will you accomplish more as a district, but you will empower others in the process.

Strategy 7: Make the Most Productive Use of Meeting Time

Have you ever participated in a meeting that lacked focus and direction? Typically, conversations meander through a variety of topics often for an extended period of time. Participants start to feel frustrated because the discussion appears endless while little is accomplished. These types of meetings are time consuming and dissatisfying for all and can reflect poorly on the leader's reputation.

For the most part, board members, administrators, staff, and parents want to be active participants, but this does not mean sitting in unproductive meetings. Those without purpose and structure discourage rather than encourage participation. At the same time, they are highly inefficient. As the school district leader, you should strive to find a balance between participant involvement and a smooth, efficient meeting structure.

Well-run meetings happen through careful planning, not chance. Whether you are leading your district administrative team or a school board meeting, it is important that you ensure that it is well organized and efficiently led. Here are several recommendations for conducting more productive meetings.

- Ensure that all meetings have a specific, defined purpose. Those which are too global in focus accomplish very little, if anything. You can still be collaborative while providing a very specific focus. In fact, meeting participants will be more invested if you begin the meeting by articulating a clear sense of what is to be accomplished.
- Take time to prepare an agenda that is distributed beforehand to participants. To build investment, encourage others to react to the agenda and even offer suggestions.
- Start each meeting by stating the specific goals and expected outcomes. Ensure that participants understand what needs to be accomplished and their role in the process. This will minimize off-task discussion and help focus the group.
- Manage the meeting discussion so that you allow all participants to feel part of the discussion. One of the most frustrating aspects of meetings for some participants is that one or two individuals dominate the discussion. The more you can involve each person in the substance of the discussion, the more effective the meeting. This may require that you establish certain meeting ground rules up-

front. For example, you might adopt a more rigid meeting structure where individuals raise their hands to comment or in other instances are called on by turn. Before you do, though, assess what structure makes the most sense for your situation.

- Stop the meeting periodically to summarize the discussion to that point. This is an effective way to reel in extraneous discussion. For example, it is perfectly acceptable to use this approach: "At this point, let me summarize what we have agreed to so far." Others can confirm or clarify your summary. This is a good strategy to refocus the group and move the discussion forward.

- Either take notes yourself or ask if someone else is willing to do so. These can be formal minutes or informal notes that are distributed to committee members and saved in case clarification is needed later. Remember that, once the meeting is over, all memories will be short. Minutes or notes help jump-start the discussion at subsequent meetings.

- End meetings on time. This will discourage unnecessary and unfocused discussion. It will also decrease the frustration felt by participants who are more time sensitive and tend to stay on focus.

- As the meeting ends, take a few moments to summarize what was accomplished. At the same time, note the purpose and focus of any additional meetings. This is also a good time to ensure that everyone is on the same page.

SUMMARY

This chapter began with a discussion of the complexity of the superintendency and the need for being the most efficient administrator possible. Introduced was the Myers-Briggs Type Indicator, an instrument that is useful in determining personality tendencies of individuals. This is particular important for superintendents who want to assess their personal strengths and weaknesses. The Myers-Briggs information is also helpful in better understanding why others act as they do. By knowing this information, you are more prepared to enhance your personal efficiency and that of the school district.

In addition, a series of strategies was offered that can help you work smarter, not harder. These included practical ideas in such areas as managing mail, maximizing the efficiency of electronic communication, and minimizing the use of paper. Also discussed were creating a personal planning calendar, managing time more efficiently, and making the most productive use of meeting time.

Closing Thoughts

Serving as superintendent of schools is one of the most stressful leadership positions in public education today. At the same time, it can be one of the most satisfying. As you move into the superintendency, you will soon discover the thrill of making a difference not only for a select group of students, as you may have as a teacher or principal, but for an entire educational community. Others, including board members, teachers, staff, and parents, will look to you as the district leader who provides direction and focus. They will rely on you to be a source of enthusiasm and a catalyst for educational excellence. You will be in the unique position to build a positive school district culture ensuring school district stability for decades to come.

To accomplish this requires unique knowledge, talents, skills, and personal resilience. Leadership success does not happen by chance. Rather, it evolves from years of experience coupled with thoughtful preparation. With a better understanding of what successful superintendents do and avoid doing in their first year, you will increase your chances of succeeding as a beginning superintendent.

Moving into the Superintendency: How to Succeed in Making the Transition was written to provide just such information. It was designed to probe important topics embedded in the role of the superintendent. These included assessing whether the superintendency is a fit for you as well as critical areas of responsibility. It was built on the conviction that beginning superintendents can enhance their success if they understand and are prepared to respond to the challenges they will most likely encounter during their first year. By avoiding the most critical pitfalls, you can be a more proactive district leader who truly makes a difference in the lives of children.

References

Bradbury, T., and Greaves, J. 2009. *Emotional intelligence 2.0.* San Diego, CA: Talent Smart.

Braun, B. 2010. *Illinois school law survey.* 10th ed. Springfield, IL: Illinois Association of School Boards.

Briggs Myers. 1993. *Introduction to type: A guide to understanding your results on the Myers-Briggs type instrument.* 5th ed., revised by L. Kirby and K. Myers. Palo Alto, CA: Consulting Psychologists Press.

Collins, J. 2001. *Good to great: Why some companies make the leap. . . and others don't.* New York: HarperCollins.

DuFour, R. 2007. In praise of top-down leadership. *The School Administrator,* November 1, 38–42.

Fielder, F. E. 1967. *A theory of leadership effectiveness.* New York: NY: McGraw-Hill.

Hunt, J., S. Watkins, T. Kersten, and J. Tripses. 2011. Restructuring (retooling) superintendent leadership programs to enhance district leadership. *Educational Leadership Review Special Issue: Portland Conference* 12(3): 43–48.

Kersten, T. A. 2006. Principal selection processes: Best practice for superintendents. In *Unbridled spirit: Best practices in educational administration,* ed. F. L. Dembowski and L. K. Lemasters. Lancaster, PA: Pro>Active Publications.

———. 2008. Teacher hiring practices: Illinois principals' perspectives. *The Educational Forum* 72(4): 355–68.

———. 2010a. Using a group interview process in teacher hiring. *The School Administrator* 67(8): 36–37.

———. 2010b. *Stepping into administration: How to succeed in making the move.* Lanham, MD: Rowman & Littlefield.

Kowalski, T., R. McCord, G. Peterson, I. Young, and N. Ellerson. 2010. *The American school superintendent: 2010 decennial study.* Lanham, MD: Rowman & Littlefield.

Marzano, R. J., and J. T. Waters. 2009. *School district leadership that works: Striking the balance.* Bloomington, IN: Solution Tree Press.

Myers and Briggs Foundation. 2010. *My MBTI personality type.* Retrieved from www.myersbriggs.org/my-mbri-personality-type.

National Center for Educational Statistics. 2009. *Fast facts.* Retrieved October 24, 2010 from nces.ed.gov/fastfacts/display.asp?id=84.

Polka, W., and P. Litchka. 2008. *The dark side of educational leadership: Superintendents and the professional victim syndrome.* Lanham, MD: Rowman & Littlefield.

Sigford, J. L. 2005. *Who said school administration would be fun?* Thousand Oaks, CA: Corwin Press.

About the Author

Thomas A. Kersten is professor emeritus in educational leadership at Roosevelt University in Chicago and Schaumburg, Illinois. He has served as an Illinois school administrator for twenty-eight years in the roles of assistant principal, elementary school principal, middle school principal, assistant superintendent, and superintendent. He is also the author of *Stepping into Administration: How to Succeed in Making the Move*, which focuses on helping new administrators make the transition from teaching to school administration successfully.

48861289R00075

Made in the USA
Lexington, KY
15 January 2016